W9-BJV-059

Alzheimer's with My Mother, Eilleen

Alzheimer's with My Mother, Eilleen

Jim Dicke II

Orange *frazer* Press
Wilmington, Ohio

ISBN for soft cover version: 978-1939710-963
ISBN for hard cover version: 978-1939710-888

Published for the author by:
Orange Frazer Press
P.O. Box 214
Wilmington, OH 45177
Telephone: 937.382.3196 for price
and shipping information.
Website: www.orangefrazer.com

Book and cover design: Alyson Rua and Orange Frazer Press

Library of Congress Control Number: 2018953796

Second Printing

CONTENTS

Alzheimer's with My Mother, Eilleen

CHAPTER 1

Why This Book?

In 1984, a friend suggested I read a small book about dementia titled "Chronicle of My Mother" by Yasushi Inoue. My father's mother was in a nursing home and was descending into dementia. She would sit holding a doll my sister-in-law had given her and seemed to find some comfort with the doll, rocking and humming. The burden of coordinating her care fell to my dad's younger sister, Mary, who lived nearby. Grandma loved books. She was a quiet and loving person, deeply loyal to her deceased husband, and parents; loving to her children, grandchildren and great grandchildren. Grandma never criticized men, but had no problem suggesting improvements for women. Her somewhat unique view on all that would make us smile. Even as she served, without pay, as our family company's corporate secretary for many years, she never actually came to the office, even a single time. She was a strong woman, but now, Grandma would act out, saying unpleasant things with a very accusatory tone. Her personality seemed different. Reading Mr. Inoue's book gave me a measure of understanding and acceptance for what she and the family would face. I hope this book can also serve a similar purpose for others.

Alzheimer's is an illness where the causes are difficult to quantify and family members may be uncomfortable with characterizations, especially in the absence of a definitive diagnosis.

While this story is primarily about my mother, Eilleen, and her struggle following an Alzheimer's diagnosis, my mother's story cannot be separated from Dad's. From her death in January 2015, he lived on to November 2016, just in time to see the election results, celebrate my birthday, and then "pass" late in the day on Veteran's Day, November 11, knowing that one of his grandson Jim III's friends had been the Veteran's Day speaker at Culver (where Dad was an honorary graduate). Dad had, for example, his own memory issues. At one stage, he initiated an earnest conversation with me. There was something he had always wanted me to know. He believed, he said, that I had never been adequately compensated for the tremendous job I had done building the company for Mr. Larsh. What started with me being mystified about what Dad was talking about, suddenly clicked. Dad thought he was speaking to his own father who died at age 50 in 1952, as opposed to the 70-year-old son sitting before him. My grandfather, Carl Dicke, had spent the larger part of his working career at the Master Electric Company in Dayton, Ohio whose major owner was Mr. Everett "E.P." Larsh. I said "Yes, Dad, I am sure that is right about your dad, Carl." I could see the realization of what he had just said cross his eyes. There were a number of moments like this and more.

Dad's paternal grandfather, Henry Dicke, had died when Dad was 16 of what was then called "premature senility." Dad's own mother, Irene Dicke, was characterized as having her brain function affected by small strokes. As with most families, medical records, if they exist at all, are no longer available. The hereditary aspects of dementia are still tentative. Even though the understanding of the medical community was less advanced just a short time ago, and tremendous progress has been made, a true understanding of the issue is still in an early stage.

At the time my mother's sister, Dorothy, died, she was not experiencing memory challenges. Mother's last living sibling, her sister Doris, is in a senior facility and does have dementia challenges, while still expressing a continued sense of humor and mischief she shared with my mother. Most tragically, Mother's youngest sibling, my uncle Warren, died of what is probably most accurately characterized as complications of Alzheimer's. Warren actually died before Mother in 2011. He was 76. Mother was never told her brother had died. It is especially important for Alzheimer's patients to avoid hurtful subjects that will hasten their own decline. As a youngster, my uncle had been nicknamed "Sunny." "Not," his mother said, "because he was a 'son', but because of his 'sunny' personality." When he developed dementia, his descent was more rapid than had been the case with my mother. He actually died of injuries that were dementia related, but really the product of a wheelchair accident. It happened like this... While in a wheelchair, he bent over to adjust his footrest as a therapy nurse had just illustrated. When he lost his balance and fell forward out of the wheelchair, the dementia had left him unable to make the reflexive moves people make to try to break or deflect a fall. He fell directly on his head and died as a result of the trauma. The nurse had been trying to divide her attention between several patients and overlooked the possibility that Warren needed a seatbelt in his wheelchair. These are some of the classic challenges our caregivers and families face every day.

My mother's mother was a different story. Grandma Webster was a smoker who struggled with undiagnosed bipolar issues most of her life. There had been one failed attempt at using shock therapy to help Grandma, but mostly she lived by willpower. She exerted an amazing effort to make each day a good day. Mostly, she succeeded. Late in life, she had medication for her bipolar disorder for the first time in her life and got that relief just as she developed dementia. Grandma also struggled with emphysema after decades of smoking. I actually believe her life was probably extended a bit by the dementia. She forgot she was a smoker, or at least was told she had given up smoking if she asked for a cigarette. Grandma's dementia mantra became, "I love you, honey" which she repeated to family members over and over. I had never heard her use the phrase when she was younger. Grandma Webster had always been an insightful judge of people, but she had never been a person who expressed love openly.

I want to especially pay tribute to my friend, Mark Bernstein. Mark has a facility to write, organize and interview that is quite special. When Mother died, I had the distinct feeling that there was information in my mother's experience that might be overlooked and lost, but also might be helpful to others. I recalled how the Inoue book had helped me. Mother was not a vain person, but as a young woman in the 1950s had abused diuretics for a time in the name of keeping her slender figure. Was this an important piece of information? Mother had a practice of taking a vitamin iron supplement, and after a hysterectomy in the 1950s, she continued to take it. As a consequence, later in life she had accumulated an excessive amount of iron in her blood profile and needed to not only stop the supplement, but to avoid certain foods like spinach for years until her iron returned to more normal levels. Clearly, there were lessons in Mother's life for family and caregivers, but were there also unrecognized hints in Mother's life story for the professional scientist? It struck me as important to at least gather the information and interviews promptly before other memories faded. Mark's interviews and organization of the material was a wonderful start.

The nursing staff kept careful records and, as a consequence, there are years of detailed records about Mother's moods, food, bodily functions, and hour by hour physical developments. Each shift of caregivers could see what had come before. The records could give Mother's doctors information, in as much detail as they cared to evaluate, and also could be there for any potential scientific research. I suspect Mother's care and moods may be more documented than any other Alzheimer's patient has been. The truth is always helpful.

The small town where they lived sometimes has an overactive rumor mill. While caregivers were systematically asked not to speak about their work with Mother and Dad, I felt a certain personal responsibility to be candid with people, while also not going into graphic detail. When asked, I would sometimes retreat into candid, but unspecific rhetoric. I would say, "It is not an easy time. We are so grateful for the really special caregivers who have become like family." I would be truthful and tried to be responsive to the inquiries, but I did not mention Dad's near blindness or Mother's verbal threats. I am sure caring friends totally understood. While I had been "speaking through the flowers" as the old German expression goes, I felt the accurate records might be helpful for some undefined purpose.

Now comes a confession. My longtime friend and personal assistant, Julie, would read the daily reports and bring to my attention only those things she thought I would need to know for me to react to developments with Mother and Dad. As the disease progresses, the type of help required becomes an always-moving target. I asked Julie if she could do this after it became clear that I found reading the daily reports myself just too much of an emotional experience. My parents were strong, smart, good and caring people. They had sometimes made mistakes; but were loving, with each other always first, but also with their two sons and their extended family as well. Reading daily about their fading selves was too hard and the wonderful Julie made my part possible. Thank you, Julie!

Following Mother's death, I felt Mark Bernstein would be best equipped to review the records, talk with the doctors and caregivers and assemble my mother's story, not as a story of her life as much as a story of her illness. I judged, perhaps incorrectly, that many would be more candid with Mark than with a family member who might have apparent pain with the subject or opinions of their own. I am extraordinarily grateful that so many spoke to Mark with such candor.

It was tricky to intrude on my parents' relationship with each other as their health declined. There are times where the child must become the parent. Both Mother and Dad were strong people who had a strong sense of boundaries and who had a strong well-defined history with each other. It is not well known, but Richard Nixon asked Dad to come to China with him on a post-presidential visit at the request of the Chinese government, to discuss business opportunities. With no hesitation, Dad said, turning down Nixon's invitation, "I don't go anywhere without Eilleen." I think that sums up their relationship. Beginning in the 1970s, Mother did not even go to the hair salon (they jokingly called it "The Hair House") without Dad. Even as a child, I recall them doing much with other couples, but activities like Mother's "ladies only" afternoon bridge club was something of an anomaly, and even that bridge club had been short lived.

Dad was a remarkable judge of people, a strong-willed, well-grounded businessman, and a good person. When it fell to me to talk with such a man about giving up his driver's license, I knew I had to be prepared for conversations about driving golf carts on state highways. Dad was a tenacious debater. When neither Mother nor Dad could sleep well together with the constant presence of caregivers in the room, I was surprised at how quickly Dad agreed it was time to move to another bedroom nearby. He never lost his capacity to respond properly to a good plan.

It is not surprising that Dad had a hard time coming to an acceptance about Mother's mental decline. They were both in a very solid denial for too long. Dad, I believe, understood that they were facing a difficulty, but his default position was always to give Mother what she wanted. In this case, she wanted to deny there was a problem. People who are accustomed to a certain amount of control over their lives and people who especially like that control, find the thought that control might be slipping away to be intolerable. Who can blame them? While it is true that an early diagnosis can help with medications to slow the progression of symptoms, it is also difficult to accept such a life-shattering diagnosis. Dad simply adored Mother. She was the enforcer. He could be the pushover. Together, they were a force of nature.

As Alzheimer's Disease progresses, needs change, dramatically and continually, while the disease and other challenges progress and intensify. A time comes when nutrition and a balanced diet are no longer important. The focus has to be on giving the patient what sustenance they will accept. In her final stages, a caregiver was literally encouraging Mother to have small bites of food and small sips of fortified liquids all day long. She lived for a time on a diet of banana cream pie and later on mini muffins. Retaining the abilities to swallow and sip a straw became serious imperatives. Knowing this is your future is hard to accept.

Dad always protected Mother, perhaps even to excess. After dropping out of college, he worked in the engineering department of a Dayton, Ohio, company. As he and Mother married, they first owned a small house in Dayton which they rented when he went into the Army Air Corps. The renters created much damage at the house during their years away and Dad was so protective, he would not even let Mother see what had become of it when they returned from the service. He disposed of the contents, including many wedding gifts, and sold the property without wanting her to even see what had happened. This was pretty standard behavior for them.

I will resist the temptation to thank people individually who were instrumental in the creation of this book and the care for my parents, because there is no way I would ever be able to thank all the right people without overlooking some who may even have been especially key. Given the age we live in, first names only are used wherever possible to protect the identity of individuals. Let me just say our family will always be grateful for all those who touched Dad's and Mother's lives. The friends, family, colleagues, caregivers and even the casual acquaintances meant everything to these two loving people.

CHAPTER 2

Eilleen and Jim

In July 1952, the peaches on our tree at 107 North Franklin Street ripened beautifully. Our home was in New Bremen, Ohio, whose perhaps 1,400 residents were then almost exclusively German in heritage and conservative in outlook. Many older homes were of a local brick, whose characteristic slightly yellowish cast reflected the nature of the local clay. Our home had been built in the 1840s and was purchased by Dad for $2,200.

The town's people had a commitment to industriousness and a dislike of waste. It is said, the town's German-American population did not work constantly. They only worked "from 'can' to 'can't'." Every small town has its story. The New Bremen story has always been a mixture of farm life and industry. The town site was chosen because it was the high point on the proposed route for the Miami-Erie Canal. The canal made the town something of a center for the early pork packing industry and then later, a local brand of wool blanket. A few case trucks were made in New Bremen; and by the 1940s, the major industries were companies that made rubber gloves, steel coil slitting machinery and a local full-service creamery. It has always been a tidy town with a healthy tax base; a family community, where the residents look out for one another.

Our home at 107 North Franklin was then the home of Mother, Dad and James II, their first-born son. I was then known as Jimmie; and, during my business life, would become known locally as Jim II (pronounced Jim Two). While Dad's ancestors had been among the early New Bremen arrivals when the town was founded, my parents were not precisely natives. Dad had been born in Ilion, New York, where his father had been working for the Remington Arms Company. His parents, Carl Dicke and Irene Kamman Dicke, had both been raised in New Bremen, but lived in New York and New Jersey following their marriage, returning to New Bremen only for their son Jim's fourth grade school year before moving to Dayton, Ohio and Carl's principle career as he became an executive with the Master Electric Company. It was in Dayton where Dad met Mother (Eilleen Webster); and the couple did not make New Bremen their home until they moved there in 1945 to join a new company founded there by Grandpa Dicke and Grandpa's brother. The company, which eventually became Crown Equipment Corporation, was, at first, a sales distributorship for thermostatic controls. So, by the standards of New Bremen, while Mother and Dad, were not exactly aliens, they were not entirely locals, either.

Dad's grandmother, Emma Mauer Dicke, lived nearby, and mentioned to Mother that those ripening peaches should not go to waste. Mother decided she probably should can them, but canning anything was not a task she had ever tried. That evening, Dad arrived home from work to encounter a kitchen of boiling peaches and a crying wife. He calmly assessed the scene, went to the garage, located an axe, went to the side yard, and chopped down the peach tree. New Bremen had its priorities. Dad had his own. Mother broke into giggles and then peals of laughter at what Dad had done, the stove was turned off, and the three of us went to a local restaurant for dinner. The peach tree story became a classic in the Dicke house; but, more importantly, it illustrates what Mother and Dad's relationship was all about. If Mother was upset about something, Dad fixed it. The solution was not always carefully considered, and it might even be abrupt. The solution might not be elegant, but the issue got fixed, and it got fixed immediately.

CHAPTER 2

My parents met as adolescents. With the directness of youth, Dad brought himself to Mother's attention by launching a chalkboard eraser in her direction while she was working a geometry problem at the blackboard of the Dayton school they both attended. As a teenager, Mother was tall, with an open face, bright eyes, and a wide smile, framed by shoulder-length brown hair. She and Dad both attended Dayton's Stivers High, where she was a member of the Homecoming Queen's Court. Mother and Dad were each other's date to the school's formal dance their senior year.

My parents' early courtship consisted of movies. For twenty cents or a quarter you saw a double feature plus cartoons. As often as not, Dad would pick a Three Stooges film, followed by a stop at a nearby A&W for ten-cent foot-long hot dogs and root beer. After high school, Mother enrolled at Miami University in Oxford, Ohio. Dad spent a year somewhat indifferently studying engineering at Ohio Northern University in Ada, Ohio, before deciding that college was less interesting than Mother. When he was not driving to see Mother, he and his pals would get familiar with Columbus, Lima, and points in between. Later in life, he regretted not having been a more serious student. The summer after Mother's second year at Miami, Dad proposed, she accepted, and the pair planned to wed on Valentine's Day, February 14, 1942. Mother's father had not been deeply enthusiastic about the timing. He had hoped Mother would complete college. When Dad sought his would-be father-in-law's blessing, Warren Webster asked if his daughter's suitor knew what marriage entailed. Dad answered affirmatively. Webster stated, "Well, I don't think you do; but, if you want to go ahead, you have my blessing."

Mother always cherished memories of her time at Miami. She had joined a sorority and made great friends. When a group of the girls decided that they would nickname themselves Snow White and the Seven Dwarfs, they chose Mother to be the character "Doc." For years, she had a little ceramic figure of "Doc" on her dressing table. Yet Mother never expressed a single regret at dropping out of college to marry Dad.

Japan's December 7, 1941 bombing of Pearl Harbor became the defining fact in the lives of millions who previously could not have found that American naval base on a map. Following Pearl Harbor, Dad gave the matter some thought; perhaps, in the circumstances, they should postpone the wedding. He sought the counsel of his father-in-law to be. Grandpa Webster replied, "If you change your mind every time the government makes a decision or changes its mind, you're going to have a tough time figuring out what to do." The wedding planning proceeded.

Whatever his advice to Dad, Grandpa was perfectly comfortable with the idea that his daughter might change her mind. Mother and Grandpa were seated in the automobile that was ready to take them to the ceremony. Mother later told an interviewer, "Daddy was just as calm as anything. We sat there and he said, 'Now, are you sure you want to go through with this?' and I said, 'Well, sure, Daddy. What if I said no? What would you do?' and he said, 'We'd just go home.' He was serious." She, too, was serious, so father and daughter proceeded to the St. John Evangelical and Reform Church in Dayton, where the couple was joined in matrimony by the Reverend Gruenwald. After a one-day honeymoon in Columbus, Ohio, Dad returned to work at the Master Electric Company.

On February 13, 1943, one day shy of their first anniversary, Dad was inducted into the United States Army Air Corps at Ft. Hayes, Ohio. He was dispatched to St. Petersburg, Florida for basic training. With that training nearing completion, Private Dicke was granted a two-week "compassionate leave" to return to Ohio, where his father had suffered a heart attack. That heart attack, as much as anything, changed the course of my father's life. The reason was that upon his return, Dad learned that the fellow members of his basic training class had completed their training and were headed to Europe. Likely, he would have to repeat basic training from the beginning. The only alternative, he was told, was that he could apply to Officers' Candidate School (OCS). The officer explaining this said the option didn't make much sense, as the application deadline was 5 p.m. that day, in just three hours. Dad said, "I don't know why it doesn't make sense; give me the paperwork.'" Dad completed the paperwork, filed it by the deadline, and found himself at OCS.

Over the next thirty months, Dad had postings throughout Texas, the Southwest, and California. First, he went to Las Vegas, Nevada for aerial gunnery training; then, six months in Amarillo, Texas, focused on the mechanics of the B-17 bomber. While there, his character and efficiency as a soldier were both rated "Excellent." Dad had grown up. From Texas, Dad went to Camp Kearns, Utah, thence to Sheppard Field, Texas, where he qualified as a sharpshooter with an M-1 carbine, and then to Santa Ana, California, for pre-flight bombardier training. Here again, his overall military performance was deemed "Excellent." The next post was Carlsbad, New Mexico. At Carlsbad, now 2nd Lieutenant Dicke completed the course of study that qualified him to be a bombardier instructor in charge of training cadet pilots in the use of the Norden bombsight, the best such instrument any country produced during the war. Simultaneously with his assignment as an instructor, Dad was doing secret work for the Office of Strategic Services. His task was to write a weekly letter to a fictitious aunt at a post office box in Grand Central Station, New York City to report if he had spotted anything of a suspicious nature. Every seven days he sent his "aunt" a letter reporting, "Nothing suspicious here."

The remarkable thing is that when Dad went into the military, Mother decided to go as well. When she learned of his posting to Amarillo, she told him, "I'll be right there." She did this despite substantial restrictions on wartime travel. Posters in every train station posed the admonitory question, "Is This Trip Really Necessary?" Restrictions could be bent, as it happened, for a young and attractive wife whose only agenda for travel was to be near her armed-services husband. Mother got herself, her clothing, and the various paraphernalia of early married life to Texas, where she found a job and off-base housing, so she could be with her husband when possible. Then, when Dad's next transfer came through, she would pack and do it again, organizing yet another home and life for the two of them. For two years, she followed his postings, leaving a trail of anecdotes in her wake. Each time he would get travel orders, neither of them would know where he was going until he arrived and could send a message. Lucky for them both, the next posting was always in the southwest United States, but they would never know where he was going until he had arrived.

The best story is from their time in Texas. One morning after Dad had left for the base, Mother answered a low but insistent knocking at the back door to discover a man wearing nothing but shoes and his underwear. He confessed that he had been paying a personal call on the lady next door; when her husband unexpectedly arrived home, he had bolted out the back. He was in considerable distress. He appealed to Mother for help: "I don't have any clothes. How am I going to get back to the base?" Mother fetched some of her husband's clothes, so he could make his return.

But there was a larger problem. The unexpected guest announced that in addition to abandoning most of his clothing, he had left his dog tags and wallet behind. The wallet could be replaced, but losing one's dog tags (the necklace that was the military's universal form of identification) was a serious offense. The next morning, Mother waited until her neighbor's husband had gone to the base. She then dropped by to see the neighbor and said, "By the way, you know you have your friend's wallet and you have his dog tags. Could you give them to me to have them returned?" That, the neighbor said, was out of the question. Her infuriated husband was waiting for the interloper to return to collect his things.

Mother said, "You give them to me. Tell your husband the MPs (Military Police) came by and insisted that you hand them over." Given a straw to grasp, the neighbor seized it and turned the dog tags, wallet, and remaining clothing over to Mother, who saw to their return. She could think on her feet. Mother had a way of impressing people. I remember when I was about fifteen years old, we went to all the places where she and Dad had been stationed. We saw so many people who remembered her so well. The trip was a joyous string of stories, places, and old friends.

On the morning of July 16, 1945, Dad drove into Carlsbad, New Mexico. He had parked his car and was standing beside it, when what looked to be a second sunrise appeared rather peculiarly located on the western horizon. Hundreds witnessed something similar. That day, the commander of the Alamogordo, New Mexico, military base issued a statement:

> Several inquiries have been received concerning a heavy explosion that occurred on the Alamogordo Air Base reservation this morning. A remotely located ammunition magazine containing a considerable number of high explosives and pyrotechnics exploded. There was no loss of life or injury to anyone, and the property damage outside of the explosives magazine was negligible. Weather conditions affecting the content of gas shells exploded by the blast may make it desirable for the Army to evacuate temporarily a few civilians from their homes.

The statement was a cover. Though he did not know it at the time, Dad had been a witness to the world's first atomic explosion, the test blast at the Alamogordo Bombing and Gunnery Range, which, though it took place a good one hundred miles from where he was standing beside his car, was nonetheless visible. It may have even been the reason for his letters to the fictitious aunt. Dad did not know what he had seen, but he knew from the size of the explosion that the information release was some kind of cover story.

Japan's formal surrender followed six weeks later. The war was over. Dad was formally discharged from his country's service on November 8, 1945. Just after his discharge, Dad and Mother's first child, I (James Frederick Dicke II) was born at 3:46 pm on November 9, 1945 in the San Angelo, Texas hospital. Mother wanted her son to have his father's name, just as her brother had his father's name. Mother's dear sister Dorothy, barely twenty years old, came to assist. Two weeks later, we all flew home on a DC-3. With black eyes from a forceps delivery by Captain MD Ian Luke, I slept the whole way on the plane's floor in a basket.

CHAPTER 3

Eilleen's Family

Mother followed Dad to war because she knew what she wanted, married life and a family, and she had decided that they would always be together as much as possible. Married life, family, and the marks of a settled life is the sort of life sought by someone whose own upbringing had been unsettling. Like her father, Mother always worried about things.

Mother's father, Warren Webster, was more than sufficiently steady. He was the son of a farmer, who was raising the fundamental Ohio crops of corn and wheat on a quarter-section farm southeast of Springfield, Ohio. When his father died in 1905 at age 28, Warren was five. His mother shortly thereafter moved to Dayton, Ohio where she opened, operated, and supported the family with a modest boarding house at 15 Davis Avenue on the city's then thriving east side. It was a bold move for a young widowed single mother. Boarding houses did not always have good reputations, even though her home's business was more about serving meals to local factory workers, than it was about renting rooms.

His mother remarried and Grandpa was just entering high school, when his new step-father gave Grandpa the option of continuing his education or going to work. Grandpa thought his step-father was telling him it was time to find a job. He was just fourteen.

Grandpa Webster had, in fact, about as much education as was common to the time, when Americans generally believed that the ability to rightly add a column of figures, write the occasional letter, and read the Bible and a few other works was about all that was required. The United States had nearly the highest literacy rate in the world. More important, he had the advantage of leaving school when Dayton, Ohio itself was something of a classroom. The booming city was drawing in workers with employment for the ambitious, opportunities to learn, and few questions asked about credentials.

For the next few years, Grandpa undertook a self-directed apprenticeship in the technical aspects of manufacturing. He was someone who became bored with any job that had nothing further to teach him. Grandpa Webster, in succession, machined railway parts for Manufacturers Production Company, undertook simple toolmaking at the Vulcan Tool Company, learned something about drafting at the Cincinnati Milling Machine Company, and folded boxes for the McLaren Cone Company, which made ice cream cones. He supplemented such efforts with night school classes at the Sinclair School in mechanical drawing, machine design, and tool design. He worked intelligently, looking for ways to improve production rather than merely meet an acceptable standard. Grandpa had an independent streak. He was more interested in getting on with the job than in getting along with fellow employees if they did not share the same interest. He loved the Horatio Alger novels. Once, when fellow workers went on strike, he put a rock in each of his jacket pockets and walked through the picket line. In 1917, at age sixteen, he took a job at the Davis Sewing Machine Company in hopes of working his way into the engineering department. Webster remained there seven years, by far his longest employment to date, becoming something of an expert on Davis' bicycle product.

During his years at Davis, Warren met and courted Mary Adams, the middle child and only redhead in a family of nine. Courtship was simple and low-key. They went to movies, or to the city's Triangle Park for dancing. A family member described Grandma as "a bit of a tomboy and a bit of a flirt." When she cut her hair in a fashionable bob, Grandpa nicknamed her "Buster" because he thought she look like "Buster Brown" in the shoe advertisement. The nickname stuck long after the hair style had gone. Grandma was just old enough to vote in the first election where women could vote. She was proudly a member of the new independent generation of women.

Both were young, determined, and in love. Determination overcame whatever reservations Mary's parents may have had about a couple marrying so young. The would-be bride and groom were both nineteen; therefore, the consent of Mary's parents was required. In November 1920, the couple wed in a quiet ceremony. The quiet did not last long. On July 1, 1921, Mary gave birth to the first of the couple's eventual four children and named her Winifred Eilleen Webster (my mother). Mary wanted her daughter to at least have her dad's initials. She was only briefly a Winifred. The uncommon double-L in her middle name was the spelling used on a piece of piano sheet music that was a favorite of Mary's. Mother was a warm engaging person, even as a child. She never went by Winifred. She always went by Eilleen.

Abruptly, the Davis Sewing Machine Company went bankrupt, following a stock manipulation. Grandpa was suddenly unemployed and Mary was expecting twins. Grandpa took a job with the jack-building company Joyce-Cridland. One assignment led to another, and a decade later, Grandpa was the company's one-third owner.

Grandpa Webster had wisdom. Family, colleagues and friends regularly turned to him for advice. He was a person who never volunteered corrections; but if you asked, he would always have a meaningful observation about the key question at hand. His two partners at Joyce Cridland gave Grandpa what they called "Warren's Pocket Veto." Even if they might disagree, they wanted Grandpa controlling the pocketbook.

Grandma Webster's second pregnancy did not go smoothly, an omen, perhaps, of things to come. Labor came early and brief.

The first twin, Dorothy, was born before the physician arrived; the second, Doris, presented as a breech birth and was pulled by the doctor into the larger world on November 7, 1925.

Mother was a lively, spontaneous and somewhat overdirecting child. Not long after the twins were born, she arrived home with her entire kindergarten class in tow. She wanted to show her friends the babies. Mary was cautious about dangers to health, so the babies were taken to a window and Mother's classmates got to view them from there. When Grandma was in the mood, she was a whirlwind of energy. And when she wasn't in the mood, she became depressive and difficult. In 1925, manic depression had not yet been defined.

Mental illness rarely draws a clear line. Manic depression, also known as bipolar disorder, might exhibit symptoms as early as adolescence; more commonly, they do not manifest until one's mid-twenties or later. The individual may just be seen as moody; the family ignores the symptoms, making allowances or excuses. Loved ones can be enablers. Often, by the time a formal diagnosis is made, the person has been afflicted with the condition for years.

Unsettled on the home front, and in the midst of a struggling national economy, Grandpa continued to manage some economic progress. In 1935, the Webster family moved to a new home. Mother, like her mother before her, began the piano lessons she would pursue for a half dozen years. Soon, the home also boasted its own telephone. In the evenings, the family listened to the radio; Grandma preferred Charlie McCarthy, Grandpa liked Will Rogers. Favorite musicians included Paul Whiteman, Lawrence Welk, and Kate Smith.

Below this normal surface, problems brewed. The move to the new home proved difficult for Grandma. Greater difficulty followed with the birth of her final child and only son. It was a very difficult pregnancy. Falling down a flight of stairs at home six weeks before her due date, she suffered a ruptured placenta. She spent her remaining pregnancy hospitalized. Warren II's birth on July 16, 1935 entailed a fifteen-hour labor that endangered both mother and newborn. Considerable blood transfusions were required. Grandpa described the event in terms that give a window on mid-1930s medical practice.

> "They had us on a table in the hospital basement. They had a tube running into a glass jar that looked like a tall water glass. I sat there and watched my blood run into the glass with the saline solution. When they got done with that, they put a napkin over the top and the nurse took the blood up and poured it into the I.V. glasses up there and gave it directly to Mary and the baby—50 ccs to the baby and 500 ccs to Mary. That was the way they did it then. The only thing they checked in those days was to see if their blood was compatible to mine."

Grandma never entirely recovered from this set of experiences. She would be on even keel for a time, then plunge into a depression. No one around her really understood her condition; nor, for that matter, did Grandma herself. Some, trying to be "helpful," would simply urge her to "snap out of it." Her family came to believe the best course was simply to step lightly around things, enjoy her good times and bear up with the bad. For Mother, then fifteen, her mother's condition brought a new role; largely, she became the surrogate mother to her twin sisters, four years her junior, and her baby brother. The twins also felt that they were raising their brother.

Successful in business, Grandpa Webster remained at a loss as to how to help his wife's distress and the hurt it caused others. Grandma's sister Ada was a nurse who worked for Dr. Thomas Addison McCann, a homeopath considered among Dayton's most esteemed physicians. Dr. McCann urged that Grandma become a patient at the Sawyer Sanitarium in Marion, Ohio. The place was a neatly laid-out and well-landscaped forty-acre "farm" that emphasized a calm setting, good nursing care, a good diet, exercise, and arts and crafts to help restore a patient's equilibrium. The Websters took this recommendation.

The "rest cure" brought benefits. They proved to be short term gains, though Grandma continued to enjoy painting ceramics and paint-by-number sets for decades. Grandpa sought other advice and investigated other approaches for Grandma, consulting a range of physicians. The pattern was one of frustrated hope. The sad, simple fact was that in the 1930s and 40s, there was simply nothing curative that medical science had to offer the manic depressive.

In early 1941, about the time Mother's courtship with Dad was turning serious, Grandma took a pronounced turn for the worse. The Websters, taking advantage of a sudden, time-pressed opportunity, made an abrupt over-the-weekend move to a new home on Canterbury Drive. Grandma's habit was to break big tasks into smaller tasks, so she would not feel overwhelmed; but even with the help of professional movers, the abrupt relocation of her home was too much. She would never move again.

Grandma hunkered down in the home on Canterbury Drive. While she never had another major breakdown, she also never achieved entirely clear sailing. For the rest of her life, Grandma resisted any further moves. Grandma, however, did not isolate herself. She and the whole family remained close. Later, when long distance calling was still an expense, Grandma and Mother spoke on the telephone almost daily. In Dayton, Grandma regularly hosted large semi-impromptu after-church Sunday family dinners that featured roast beef. She also enjoyed Yahtzee, a dice game, with her grandchildren. The young set enjoyed her company, even though by general consent, where Yahtzee was concerned, Grandma's commitment to the rules of the game was flexible.

CHAPTER 4
Coming to Town

Mother and Dad arrived in New Bremen in November 1945, with me in tow. Dad had agreed to work for Crown Controls Company, a business just launched by his father, Carl, and an uncle. The three of us lived with the extended Dicke family in a house on Washington Street. Mother, Dad and I would share a room for some years. Grandpa Dicke had purchased the home from his wife's parents, Fred and Margaret Kamman, who lost their savings after the collapse of the local bank, with the understanding that the Kammans could also continue to live there for the balance of their lives. Dad's two sisters were also in residence.

Nine individuals from four generations lived in that house with a single bathroom, used by all except Great Grandpa Kamman, who claimed to prefer the outhouse in the backyard. From the perspective of Dad and Mother, the circumstance was an economic necessity. Dad was not initially paid for working at the company. From Mother's perspective, she might have felt crowded as one of the eight adults living in the four-generation Dicke family home. Grandpa Dicke, simply adored Mother (his daughter-in-law), and tried to do whatever was needed to make her comfortable. At least a certain German emotional restraint governed. The family was easy to be around.

Slowly, the Washington Street living arrangement changed. Dad's two sisters left for college and marriage. Dad's sister Edna, who was also my godmother, married first. I was a two-year-old ringbearer, slightly out of control. Then, Great Grandpa and Great Grandma Kamman both died within thirty days of each other. They were dear people who I had nicknamed Little Grandpa and Little Grandma. Mother, Dad and I moved to the modest brick house at 107 North Franklin Street. Dad's younger sister married in the fall of 1951. I was becoming a well-practiced ring bearer and family mascot.

In September 1952, Mother gave birth to my brother Dane, her second and final child. Three months later, Carl Dicke, Dad's father, died unexpectedly of a heart attack, only age 50. It was a blow. I was only seven when he died, but Grandpa Dicke had been my buddy and the loss, just one week before Christmas, left the entire family bereft. In some ways, Grandpa continued to be a spirit in our lives for decades.

Mother worried and was protective. She worried for friends, for family, and for loved ones. Grandpa Dicke's death brought out in Mother a protectiveness and concern for her family that may have been hard-wired into her, given the home in which she had been raised. Mother extracted a vow from Dad—he would withdraw from active business life once he reached 50; which he in fact did in 1971, the age at which his father, Carl Dicke, had died.

With his father-in-law's tutelage, Dad and Crown Controls Company Incorporated managed slowly up a very steep hill, with hard work and reinvestment of earnings. The company had certain advantages. New Bremen was a minor center of skilled metalworking. Crown drew its work force from the mechanically-inclined and improvisation-oriented farmers who surrounded the town. Farmers tend to boast a work ethic that would be the envy of almost any organization. Further, Dad's personality invited an "everyone pitches in" attitude that is a secret strength of many small businesses. Dad himself was a kind, competent, caring leader, whose personality drew people to his team. At one point, with the company scrambling to fill a rush order, work hours were extended and Mother lent support by shuttling batches of sandwiches and hot coffee from home to those working under the deadline. Mother was willing to be supportive of the business effort in every way.

To save money, Mother sewed. Her younger brother was but ten years older than her eldest son, so she cut down some of her brother's castoffs for me to wear, sewed other items, and went to particular lengths to make me a winter overcoat. Unfortunately, her brother's winter clothing would often fit me in the summer and vice versa.

Mother's engagement with the business was indirect. Like Grandma Dicke, Mother never went to the office, but she was always ready to be supportive. Dad and Mother would attend trade shows and Mother always assumed the role of gracious hostess and company first lady. Her advice, when it came, frequently reflected her instincts for people. She was, said her grandson, Jim Dicke III, "a person who knew who she liked and who she didn't like." It was advice Dad almost always took.

Their partnership produced remarkable results. With the proceeds of Grandpa Dicke's $25,000 life insurance policy, my grandmother purchased machine tools she could lease to the company. The income from parts produced on those machines bought more machines, and Crown grew by making products for the new television industry. By 1955, the company was doing one million dollars in annual sales volume.

Then, at Grandpa Webster's suggestion, Crown started producing a little hydraulic stacker for moving tools in machine shops. One product became more products; and, through the 1960s, the company expanded its product offerings, developed dealer relationships and where that was not possible, opened sales offices. By 1968, the company was doing ten million dollars a year in sales volume.

Through the years, their dream was about building a company to pass along to the next generation. They were never tempted by the wealth they might have had by selling the company.

Mother may never have gone to the office; but, for them, each day was a loving partnership. Ronald Reagan would later open more doors for private companies to borrow working capital; but in the 1950s and 1960s, it was difficult to grow a business while keeping the business private. Mother and Dad built a remarkable success. The company continued to grow. As forklifts became the primary and then the only product, the company became Crown Equipment Corporation. By 1990, when Mother and Dad decided they could afford a yacht, sales were $400 million annually, and there were more than 2,500 employees. More recently, with over 15,000 employees and 18 factories, Crown has become one of the largest private manufacturing companies in America. Mother never seemed surprised by it all, but Dad was always amazed at what his company had become, and was so proud of the job everyone had done. His pride in his grandson Jim III was a special pleasure in his final years.

CHAPTER 5

Friends

Around 1955, Mother joined a bridge group, eight women playing at two tables. The game itself was a friendly gathering, people talked as much as they played and rarely called attention to a bad play made by their partner. Play rotated through the households of the members. Snacks were limited, and while people dressed for the event, they didn't dress up. Six decades later, one of those women, Margaret, at the time, a mother of two young children, recalls Mother vividly. "Eilleen was not the type of person who put on airs. What you saw was what you got. Beauty on the inside and beauty on the outside. Her dress was simple and elegant, never overdid the jewelry. She was a perfect listener. She always listened to me, never interrupted, and looked me or anybody straight in eye as she did it."

An even earlier memory comes from Jim Moeller, who has been a New Bremen resident his entire ninety-five years. They met as people in small towns do, by proximity and commonality. Like Dad, Moeller was a recently discharged veteran, and they shared an interest in manufacturing. Moeller worked in production control at Stamco, a well-established New Bremen firm.

Mother, Dad, Jim and Nedie Moeller, and two other couples socialized commonly, most often at a dinner one of the couples would host at home. Mother, Moeller recalled, jokingly referred to him as "Jim Honey," to distinguish him from her husband. She had, he stresses, a fine humor and a talent for putting people at ease.

Moeller's respect for Dad was such, he said, that he never risked working for him. Explaining, Moeller said, "I considered Jim a friend my whole life. Jim had the kind of powerful personality, and a way with people, he could be so persuasive that he could make people think it was a good idea to jump into the water if he asked them to do it. I wasn't sure I wouldn't do it."

Nonetheless, Mother was a worrier and inclined to concern for her sons' physical safety. Most town kids biked wherever they chose; I, however, was not to ride anywhere without getting Mother's permission.

I was a quiet and serious kid who, years later, Mother described as an old soul. She said she would watch me from the window, sitting on my tricycle when I was little, elbow on the handlebars, chin in my hand, just looking down and thinking. Mother had aspirations for us all. She was a matriarch in training. We never watched a football game on television. Mother did not want one of her sons to decide they liked any contact sport. Horseback riding and tennis were okay as sports, as were baseball and some basketball, but playing football was not allowed. Later, said her granddaughter Anastasia, Mother became concerned about "edges"—the edge of the table, the boat, the pool—"She was always concerned that grandkids were going to fall off the boat or run into a table or fall in the pool." Mother would let the grandkids go into the ocean, only up to their knees.

Concern can be prudent. As a young child, my brother Dane was a climber, who had a mind of his own. One day, he ascended the four-legged antenna tower, behind the house. Having climbed it, Dane perched and took in the view. Mother came out, spotted her son, and turned the matter over to her husband, who asked Dane if he was okay. Dane said he was. Dad said it was time to come down. Dane asked if he was in trouble. Dad said, "No, but you should come down." Later, the tower was fenced, to prevent repetitions.

Mother's sense of being "at home" in New Bremen was rather beside the point. "She was of that generation of women for whom 'being at home' was defined by whether she was with her husband and her children. Wherever she was with Dad was home."

As Dad neared the age of 50, they made an intentional effort to choose a spot in Florida to spend winters. They knew people who highly recommended this community or that; but, in the end, the very New Bremen-like small town feel of the Ocean Reef Club community on Key Largo and its easy-going informality and lack of pretention and self-importance suited them. They made life-long friends at Ocean Reef and when they took to boating in their middle sixties, they called their family yacht the "Reef Chief."

CHAPTER 6

Culver

There is a short list of locales associated with Dad and Mother. The list includes the small town of Culver, Indiana. Culver is home of the Culver Military Academy and Culver Girls Academy. This is the school attended by my brother and me, and all of the grandchildren. Culver is not one of those military academies to which errant youth are sent to get the errant sanded off. Nor is it a place where parents send their children to rid themselves of the burdens of parenthood. Mother and Dad established a modest home in Culver, generally spending alternate weekends there in the winter when their sons were students.

Dad had, as a young man, seen an advertisement for Culver in an issue of *Boy's Life* magazine. It struck him as just the sort of school he wished he could himself attend. When, as a father, those means were available, he wanted his sons to enjoy the opportunity. Culver had been founded by Henry Harrison Culver in 1894 "for the purpose of thoroughly preparing young men for the best colleges, scientific schools and businesses in America." Today, in similar terms, the school states its mission as "educating its students for leadership and responsible citizenship in society by developing and nurturing the whole individual—mind, spirit, and body—through integrated programs that emphasize the cultivation of character." Culver went co-educational in 1971. Today, the physical resources of its 1,800-acre campus and large endowment would likely be the envy of many well-regarded liberal arts colleges. Among nonacademic endeavors, the school is particularly known for its Equestrienne program and the Black Horse Troop. Both have participated in many Presidential inaugural parades.

I loved the school. At Culver, I came into my own academically. It was, indeed, a military school, with an hour-by-hour schedule that detailed where each student was supposed to be. Options were limited. If, say, you had a free hour wedged between an English class and a math class, you could spend that hour studying in your room or studying in the library. You were not free, however, to spend that hour studying by the lake. Nor, for that matter, could you listen to the radio or to record players during the day. I was not rebellious. There was not a high level of tolerance for misbehavior, but Dane and I were not there for discipline. We didn't particularly need discipline. With the seven-year age span between us, Dane and I were never students on campus at the same time.

As she aged, Mother became more meticulous. She labeled articles of clothing with a circular paper tag that gave such information as when she had last worn it and how often she had worn it. This was done, her granddaughter Jennifer noted, "So God forbid she would show up at an event and be wearing the same thing she had worn to a similar event a year ago or two years ago."

Mother bought clothes at the Billy Lewis Clothier and Boutique, located in Dayton, Ohio. Lewis' staff member Frances Smith Oxrider, generally known as "Oxi," would call Mother whenever something came into the store that she thought Mother might enjoy.

One day, Oxi suggested that Dane, then seventeen, might wish to meet Oxi's granddaughter, Cindy Thomas, a Dayton native visiting from Massachusetts. It was a slightly unusual suggestion. There was not a girl in the world good enough for her baby boy, or his older brother. Mother would say, "I'm glad I had two boys. Girls are sneaky." In the summer of 1969, Oxi and the granddaughter drove to my parents' summer place at Indian Lake. Upon arrival, Cindy apologized for being late, saying they had gotten lost. Dane, with a sort of instant familiarity, replied, "You would." The Dicke summer home on Wolf Island was not easy to find on the unmarked local roads. Dane said later, "I didn't believe in love at first sight, but that's what it was." Through the following school year, Dane's final at Culver, the couple courted through occasional visits and extensive long-distance telephone calls. The following June, Dane and Cindy were photographed, "grinning like idiots", with Dane, just graduated, in his Culver uniform. The course of true love does not always run smooth, and nearly four decades would pass before Dane and Cindy would marry.

Culver attendance may actually have helped along my own matrimony. Following graduation, I enrolled at Trinity University in San Antonio, Texas. Freshly arrived on campus, I was in a parking lot when a car carrying four women drove up. Unexpectedly, its driver stopped and asked, "Does your name happen to be Jim Dicke?" The driver was the sister of a friend from Culver who had passed word that I would be enrolling with her at Trinity, pointing out my picture in his Culver yearbook. The car's passengers included Janet St. Clair, who had grown up in Pittsburgh, and then moved to Houston when her father was transferred to Texas. Janet and I became friends. By junior year, we were dating. We became engaged our senior year, and were married the month after graduation. The marriage occurred in Texas, with Mother managing many of the details.

Mother's friend Ruth Ann Schwieterman recalled, "Eilleen had everything organized, from the outdoor dining and table cloths, to making all the appointments for guests for hair and manicures. That was the usual Eilleen—the perfect hostess, walking around with her book and all her little assignments." Mother was never a diarist, but as she aged, record keeping became more compulsive. On secretarial spiral notepads, she would record everything. Once, when a friend asked to be reminded of the name of a restaurant they had eaten at together some years earlier in a distant city, Mother consulted her notepads and reported not only the name of the restaurant, but what each of them had eaten.

Dane graduated from Culver in 1970 and also went to Trinity University in San Antonio. Carrying a briefcase in the registration line, he was taken for a graduate student by a fellow freshman girl. They talked, and then dated briefly, but Dane's own gaze shifted to her roommate, Kerry Sexton. Their dating turned to courtship and led to marriage in November 1974.

Many years later, in 2008, a classmate of mine from Culver asked me if I had a cousin named Dane; because, if so, then he had once dated a cousin of his, Cindy. I responded that I do not have a cousin Dane, but I do have a brother Dane; and, if the Cindy in question was Cindy Thomas, then she was indeed a girl my brother had dated. And so it was. At this point, both Dane and Cindy were divorced, Cindy in Florida and Dane in California. A little prospective matchmaking ensued, with me contacting Dane and my friend contacting Cindy to see if they might like to be placed back in touch. The upshot was that on Valentine's Day 2009, Janet and I shared a meal with Dane and Cindy at the Anglers Club in Key Largo, Florida. On the day before Thanksgiving in 2010, the pair who had met forty years earlier were married, still enjoying those same idiot grins.

CHAPTER 7
The Company

When Dad's father, Carl Dicke, died of a heart attack in 1952, Mother extracted a pledge that Dad would retire from business on reaching that age. In 1971, Dad honored the pledge. By title, he remained as chairman, president, and treasurer. Irene Dicke, my grandmother, was the company secretary, and Dad remained active; but, for all practical purposes, the company was thereafter run by a triumvirate consisting of myself, age 26, and two longtime associates of Dad's, Tom Bidwell and Verlin Hirschfeld, to whom, especially in the early years, I often deferred.

Tom gave Crown its emphasis on design. There was no particular reason, he believed, why a lift truck should not win awards for industrial design. Crown would win many. Further, Tom pushed the company into overseas markets. Verlin looked to the financial side, making sure we did not outrun our budgets. I learned so much from them both. Neither Tom nor Verlin had been to college. Neither, for that matter, particularly admired the other. None of this changed the fact that we all worked with considerable teamwork, creating for the company steady growth and progress. Building a company is about making good choices, and you have to accept that choosing to do one thing is also a choice not to do something else.

While Dad started spending more time away in the winter, he did not disappear. He called the office regularly, curious to know what was happening. Over the summer, he (fairly often) came to Crown headquarters in New Bremen, not so much to attend business meetings, as to do what he enjoyed—walking through the plant, chatting with those doing the work. "How's that machine running?" "Is it making good parts?" He was gracious, inquisitive, unpretentious, and with a startling recollection for faces and the people attached to them. Dad and Mother just thoroughly enjoyed people.

CHAPTER 8

Grandchildren

With marriage and time came grandchildren. My 1968 marriage to Janet led to Jim III and Jennifer, born 1971 and 1975, respectively. Dane's 1974 marriage to Kerry produced Anastasia (1975) and Robin (1979). All four spent their early years in proximity to their grandparents. When Jim III and Jennifer were growing up, Dad and Mother were also their neighbors, as Janet and I built a home next door to my parents, on one of the relatively few building lots then available in New Bremen. Dane, Kerry and their children lived in New Bremen then, as well. Mother and Dad adored their grandchildren, making time available for them was always a high priority.

As the lay of the land and the routing of streets had it, Jim III and Jennifer's shortest route to school led across their grandparents' yard. Sticking strictly to the streets produced a longer walk. Jennifer recalls, "So Gram and Gramp had somebody come and put a concrete sidewalk through their yard. My brother and I could just cut through the yard and go to school, which we thought was cool." They had also installed the sidewalk to accommodate all the neighborhood children and got pleasure out of seeing it used, even long after their own grandchildren ceased needing it.

One summer, Mother taught Jennifer and her cousin Anastasia how to tap dance. Anastasia recalls, "It was one of those whimsical things you did if you visited her in the summer. She just showed us the basics, we must have been about six. We tap danced on the porch. I remember being so excited by it all." One day, Jim III and

Jennifer asked if their grandmother would like to join them for a picnic. Mother responded, "Of course." So, as Jim III says, "Jennifer and I packed our sandwiches and went next door. Gram came out. I looked at her and said, 'Where's your lunch?' She thought that was the funniest thing. Since we'd invited her for a picnic lunch, she didn't assume the need to bring her own lunch. She was a good sport about it."

When all lived in New Bremen, the grandchildren were fairly common sleepover guests. Robin recalled staying in a bedroom down the hall from her grandparents, unable to sleep and a bit lonely. If she'd been home, she would have gone to her mother. Instead, she went to wake her grandmother. Mother, somewhat groggy, was holding a tissue in her right hand. She reached over her head, grabbed another tissue, and, giving it to Robin, told her it was a security blanket. Holding it, Robin went back to sleep.

To Jim III and Jennifer, Mother was "Gram"; to Anastasia and Robin, she was "Nana." To all, she was easy to be with. Jennifer says, "I always felt that at family gatherings, sitting right between my Gram and Gramp was the best place to be. They were super fun. And they were the life of the party." On one family trip, Jennifer recalled Gram felt the energy was dragging. "So, she looked around, found some CDs, and one of them was Willie Nelson's greatest hits. She played 'On the Road Again' at full volume for everyone to perk them up, and we sang and danced. For the next thirty years, every time we were going somewhere, getting in the car to go to dinner, or whatever, she would sing a little bit of that song. And we smiled every time." Monica, a niece, said Aunt Eilleen "always made you feel like you were a favorite. We were both Cancers, and she said, 'Oh, we're like sisters'." On one visit, Monica admired a small brass Buddha and Mother immediately gave it to her.

Mother enjoyed tennis. Jim III recalled, "During the summer when I was a kid, I'd call Gram and say, 'Want to play some tennis?' She would say, 'Absolutely.' We started doing this when I was young enough that she would routinely mop the floor with me. Then, I remember getting to a point where it was more competitive, and she started to play better. I remember thinking, 'Ah, you've been holding back.' Then, at some point, I started to beat her more than she would beat me. It didn't bother her, she thought it was great."

Acceptance was not without limits. While there were "no painted lines, there were lines." Having been told to come to visit any time, Dane's daughter, a then nine-year-old Anastasia, decided to bring a friend for a swim in her grandparents' pool. They biked over, parked their cycles, entered through an unlocked front door, collected several towels, and headed for the water. When the housekeeper came out to ask what they were doing, Anastasia responded that she had a standing invitation. But that was not, in fact, how things stood. "About five minutes later," said Anastasia, "here comes my grandmother. It was the only time in her life that I saw her really mad. I knew immediately I had done something wrong. She said I needed to know that there was protocol. While I was a welcome visitor, an advance phone call was entirely in order. She was very stern in the way she asked us to get out of the pool."

Most special of all was that grandchildren were taken in turns, one at a time, on trips with their grandparents. Jennifer recalled, "They didn't take us until we were able to dress ourselves and be responsible enough, so that at the end of the evening we could go into our own room and take care of ourselves. Usually, they would consult the child on what they wanted to do, where they wanted to go." Jennifer says, "One year all I wanted was Disney World. We went, and while there, we went out one evening to a place that had a singer. They were trying to get people to get up on the stage and sing. At first, I was too shy; but, once I started, they had trouble getting me off the stage."

When traveling, with or without grandchildren in tow, it was Mother who pushed the evening along. Jim III recalls, "At the end of dinner, she was the one who was pushing to go somewhere next.

By that point, everyone else was ready to go home and go to bed. I don't think it was just me, but my grandfather, too would go just to make her happy. We'd go listen to music. My grandfather would get to the point in the evening when he thought he'd humored her enough and he'd say, 'All right, Eilleen, you can take me home now.'" On one trip to Juneau, Alaska, everyone arrived jet-lagged but it was Gram, who was determined to visit the town's well-known Red Dog Saloon. "So, we trudged maybe ten blocks down the street; it was a cold, dark hilly walk down to the Red Dog. We took one step inside the door and it was like a scene out of a Wild West movie—loud, completely packed, everyone rowdy, a big room thick with smoke. Gram looked at it and said, 'I don't know. What do you guys think? It looks a little rough.' Gramp replied, 'Yes, a little rough.' So, we turned around and trudged back to the hotel."

CHAPTER 9

The Boat—David and Ruth Ann

Mike grew up in a boat building family in New Zealand. He chose to move himself and his range of skills to Australia. One day in 1989, he was welding below the decks of a private yacht under construction in Australia's Brisbane shipyard, when he was met with an outstretched hand and a voice that said, "You must be Mike. I'm Jim Dicke, and this is my wife, Eilleen."

The boat, then known as vessel #16, was later named the "Reef Chief."

Delivered in April 1991, the "Reef Chief" became a second home to Mother and Dad. Designed by a marine architect, the craft had twin Caterpillar engines and twin Cummins generators. The boat had a range of nearly 4,000 miles, which meant it could cross any ocean the earth had to offer. The hull and superstructure were aluminum, the decking was teak, and the main deck provided the master stateroom, an owner's office and pantry with dining area. A stairway led to the upper deck, with pilothouse and sky lounge. The lower deck contained three guest rooms. The boat would sleep eight, along with quarters for the crew. Dad finally had the wonderful boat he had always wanted.

The boat took three years to complete, double its scheduled time. The original builder went bankrupt. Mike and several others formed a company to finish the project, employing between fifteen and twenty craftsmen selected from those they knew and trusted, with the bills paid by the company that had posted the performance bond for the original builder. Dad and Mother spent the additional year-and-a-half of construction time living on the eighteenth floor of the Brisbane Hilton.

Soon, a routine was established. Mike would pick Dad and Mother up at 1 p.m., so they could check progress on the boat. "Eileen would always bring me a fresh apple and say, 'OK, Mike, here's your lunch.'"

Since it was a private boat, Mike notes, it had no goods to deliver on a schedule. The family, their safety and comfort were the prime considerations. Once, when the boat ran aground in a channel, Mother decided to declare it an event. She organized a pool on what time the tide would lift the boat free.

Mike says, "Jim might have been boss at the office, but she was the boss on that boat and at their home, and we all knew it." When Dad came in complaining about the volume at which Bob Marley songs were being played, Mother said, "We like Bob Marley. He's that guy from Jamaica." Dad responded, "Oh, okay then. I guess I was just kidding." When Mike overlooked a then-existing Crown rule against facial hair, turning up with a goatee, Dad confronted him, "What's that on your chin? I want it gone." Mike recalled, "Eileen said, 'I like it. Keep it.' So, I kept it."

Mother and Dad shared ship's quarters for several months a year with a New Bremen couple, David and Ruth Ann Schwieterman. David was a long-time friend, a pharmacist who carried a general air of mischief. Such a reputation gave David a supporting role in one of the town's more enjoyed stories. On one occasion, in all innocence, David entered the local bank simultaneously with two men who had dropped by to rob it. The tellers, seeing the purported robbers in David's company, decided some elaborate joke was in progress. Only with some difficulty were they persuaded that they were actually indeed being robbed. David brought out in Dad a certain return of his own youthful misbehavior. The pair once wandered off during a shopping expedition with their wives, and were found sitting on chairs in a display window, watching the staff change the apparel on the mannequins of a Victoria's Secret store.

David's wife, Ruth Ann, met the Dickes soon after moving to New Bremen, following her 1964 marriage to David. Ruth Ann excelled at golf, she was a skilled pianist and choir director, two activities she soon shared with Mother. The golf matches generally teed-off sometime in the early afternoon. Ruth Ann also became Mother's piano teacher, when the latter decided to improve her piano skills. Mother had other talents. She could, David attested, "shaggy dog" a story as well as anyone, mimicking the story's participants and tossing in digressions to delay the punch line. Trips on the boat were often impromptu. Ruth Ann says, "Jim would call and say, 'Want to have a little fun? When can you be ready for departure?'"

The boat would stop at Key Largo or Boca Raton, Florida, or Harbor Island and elsewhere in the Bahamas, or Caribbean. For Mother, being in port meant gathering shells from above the tide line or, more likely, scouring the local markets for knickknacks. Ruth Ann said, "When we came into port we always went to the local market, where they had booths. We would pick days when there weren't many cruise ships in port because Eilleen said that meant prices would be lower. We would buy silly hats and shirts. They were just fun days for us." While the women toured and shopped, Dad and David often remained behind on deck, reading and talking.

Days frequently ended with a cocktail hour on the boat and a good dinner ashore, often at a restaurant recommended by Mike. In one port, they frequented the Thirty-Thirty club, always sitting at Table 15, where Dad, who enjoyed music only up to a point, would sometimes slip the band's leader some cash, asking him to "Quit twenty minutes early."

They had their rituals. Mother insisted on the Sunday comics. Dad often cooked morning eggs for everybody on a little electric skillet. When, in later years, grandchildren came visiting, they might sleep on air mattresses on the deck. Their times on the boat were some of the happiest days of their lives.

CHAPTER 10
It Begins

Into her seventies, Mother remained a dedicated supporter of the local Girl Scouts. She was a routine visitor to the Girl Scout day camp and had supported the building of the regional Girl Scout headquarters building in Lima, Ohio. She was, in all likelihood, Auglaize County's leading purchaser of Girl Scout cookies, buying boxes that found their way in and around the company and the town. In 1995, she was invited to speak at an event the organization was holding. She put considerable time into her intended remarks. Once at the podium, however, her comments strayed, sentences began to ramble. Dad came to the podium, offered a brief apology, and led Mother back to her seat.

One day, long-time housekeeper, Carol, heard Mother mumbling to herself in the bathroom. Carol asked, "Eilleen, do you need some help?" Mother responded, "Yes, I do." "So, I went in and that's when I noticed she needed someone to tell her how to finish putting on her makeup. She had a staring look on her face as though she was wondering what she was supposed to do next."

Some medical events are as obvious as a fracture or as sudden as a heart attack. Dementia is far less easy to diagnose; not simply for the layman, but for the physician as well. Dementia offers no clear border of time between the "before" and "after" of onset. In part, this is because those who see someone most regularly are less likely to notice incremental behavioral changes. This is like the relative who visits least often, but is most likely to comment on how the kids have grown. For example, Ruth Ann, Mother's closest friend in New Bremen, said, "I never really felt any particular sign. She was always so joyous. David and I never came home and said, 'Eilleen really has a problem.'" As for Mother herself, she was very vocal about denying that she was having any memory problem whatsoever. She was insistent and would question why anyone would say anything so unkind. Dad would sit silently, not voicing an opinion in front of others, but privately encouraging her to work on it and try harder.

Diagnosis is further muddled by the fact that the commonest early sign of Alzheimer's symptoms is difficulty with short-term memory. In truth, some weakening of memory is a natural consequence of aging. Indeed, it has become a commonplace for individuals to refer to the temporary inability to find the name that sits right at the tip of the tongue as "a senior moment."

There are deeper waters. Alzheimer's is a diagnosis many people strongly wish to avoid, and not only those who may suffer from it. Such a diagnosis is, for the sufferer, essentially a sentence to a lingering and ever-more helpless life and an unavoidable death. It is, at the same time, often a sentence to those who love and cherish that individual, a sentence that will take their time, peace of mind, and financial security. Mother clung to denial as long as possible.

Zita, a friend of Mother's, recalled a time, maybe 1997, when Mother was unable to locate some jewelry. With increasing frustration, Mother searched through handbag after handbag. Zita said, "Eilleen, you just had it. And you put it over there." Mother gave a nod, saying she simply didn't remember. Zita commented later, "That was the first time I wondered. Other than that, she was always right there and ready to go. Her natural exuberance made it easy to overlook temporary lapses. That was the only time I ever noticed that it just didn't seem like her."

My wife, Janet, recalls a gathering in July 2000. Wishing to help with the meal, Mother went to set the table. Janet said, "She couldn't figure out how to do it. She would wipe the same spot with a wet sponge repeatedly, and could not remember how to place the utensils." Janet's reaction was to say to me, "Something even more serious is starting to happen."

In fall 2002, the Dicke Hall of Mathematics was dedicated at the Culver Academies. Jim III went to the event with his grandparents, and was helping Mother, then eighty-one, into their van. He recalled, "She got halfway into the van and she kind of lost track of where she was and started to panic badly." Where was she? Was she going to fall? She neither fell nor was she injured, but, her grandson said, "I had never seen her panic like that."

Mother also seemed unable to see for herself that something was wrong. A niece recalled a visit to Indian Lake. "She could still carry on a conversation, and she did something similar to what Grandma Webster had done. If she didn't know exactly what was being said, she could fake her way through a conversation." More distressing events occurred during the visit. The niece recalled, "At one point, everybody was outside. Aunt Eilleen was inside and she lost sight of Uncle Jim, and she just started raising her voice. She was very upset." Almost as startling was that the following morning, the invariably stylish Mother came to breakfast wearing the same clothes she had worn the night before. Even then, her niece recalled, "She was all smiles. She gave me a hug, she gave me a kiss. She was very sweet." Mother started to insist on wearing one particular favorite yellow outfit every day.

My brother Dane later reported, "I had been told that I should not be surprised when I visited. There were times when she was fine and other times when she couldn't remember." There were also times when a particular memory itself was the surprise. In May 2004, Dane was at dinner one evening, when Mother suddenly rattled off a string of numbers. Everyone fell silent. Then, Dad said, "That was my serial number in World War Two." Later in 2004, Anastasia went to hand over her child to her 'Nana' so a picture of them could be taken. Dane intervened, saying, "I don't think that's a very good idea." At that point, Anastasia recalled, "I realized something was seriously concerning."

Evidence accumulated. Mirrors began to confuse. Mother and Dad visited the Bahamas, lush with flowering vines. Mother became alarmed when a petal dropped on the path in front of her.

CHAPTER 11

The Diagnosis

Mother's neurologist, Dr. Kenneth Pugar, said, "In my day, very few people went to medical school to become a neurologist. Neurology was not a common field, it was limited by a lack of what you could do for people. Why would you want to be a neurologist? You'd make the diagnoses, but then there was very little that could be done for the people who were your patients."

But Dr. Pugar's timing was fortunate. Within five years of his entering the field, the first drug that slowed dementia was introduced. Dr. Pugar said, "We got so excited in neurology in those years as we began to understand the mechanism of the illnesses, Parkinson's disease, Multiple Sclerosis, stroke, and forms of dementia." Advances followed. The use of dopamine changed the treatment of Parkinson's disease. Anti-clotting drugs became central to the treatment of stroke. Magnetic Resonance Imaging (MRI) gave a much clearer view of what was happening with the brain.

Dr. Pugar's was the name given to me when I sought a recommendation from the Crown Equipment Corporation's physician regarding my mother. At Dr. Pugar's suggestion, it was me, and not Dad, who accompanied Mother to her assessment. The reasoning was that a spouse is often more likely to try to "sell" the physician on his or her own point of view on the matter.

A variety of tests help the physician diagnose. In one, the patient is asked to draw a clock face showing a particular time. Other tests are as simple as asking for a recitation of the months of the year backwards, starting with December. Or saying, "If you have two quarters, three dimes, and two nickels, how much money do you have?" It can be so important to have an early evaluation. The earlier the intervention, the more that can be done to slow the progression of the symptoms. If Mother had been willing, an earlier diagnosis would have been helpful. It is not unusual for someone who may suspect a problem to even decline a "baseline analysis." It is an unwise refusal.

During their first visit, Dr. Pugar asked Mother if she knew why she was there.

"You're the foot doctor," she replied, "and I've been having trouble with my feet."

Dr. Pugar responded, "Actually, Mrs. Dicke, you're here because you've been having trouble with your brain."

Employing a favorite phrase, Mother said, "Tell me about it."

CHAPTER 12
The Disease

Longer lifespans have led to the dramatic increase in Alzheimer's. The disease is strongly age-correlated. At fifty, only one individual in 2,500 is likely to contract the disease. By age eighty-five, the odds approach fifty-fifty. In short, Alzheimer's is among that class of "recent" diseases ushered on the stage with our longer lifespans. Many ailments like Parkinson's disease, amyotrophic lateral sclerosis (Lou Gehrig 's Disease) and others, once remained in a sort of waiting room because, in the past, few people lived long enough to contract them. Here, evolution failed. Over the long stretch of time, many genetic defects have been eliminated from the human gene pool because those who carried the defect were less likely to produce the fertile young that would ensure the trait in question would be retained into future generations. Evidence is strong that there is a considerable but hardly decisive genetic disposition to Alzheimer's, but people disposed to Alzheimer's will not be filtered out of the gene pool by evolution, because by the time people are suffering from the disease they have already passed through their reproductive years.

Research into Alzheimer's hit a roadblock similar to that faced by research into Acquired Immune Deficiency Symptom (AIDS). All vaccines in use, dating back to Edward Jenner's seventeenth-century discovery that infecting someone with cowpox generally protected them against the far more serious disease of smallpox, worked because giving an individual a milder form of a given disease prompted the body to produce protective antibodies. This approach failed with AIDS, because no milder form of the disease existed to provide a basis for a vaccine. A parallel problem exists with Alzheimer's. The reason is simple: the human brain is far and away the most complex creation in nature. You cannot test a possible Alzheimer's cure on an animal, because an animal's brain lacks the complexity to be given Alzheimer's in the first place.

The conversion of sense impressions to short- and long-term memory is mediated by the hippocampus, a finger-length brain segment in that lies near the front of the brain at a point somewhat higher than the ears. The hippocampus develops rather late in the progress of the brain's maturation. Two phenomena follow. First, it explains why children, particularly those under the age of four, have little memory of their own past, a state known as infantile amnesia. Second, the hippocampus is often the first region of the brain attacked by Alzheimer's.

Following the hippocampus, the amygdala often becomes compromised. Regulating emotions like fear and anger, hostile eruptions and bursts of anxiety may occur all out of proportion to events, or even out of nowhere. "Tangles spread outward through much of the rest of the brain, following the same pathways that sensory data travel in a healthy brain." The tangled neurons entwine upon each other.

In the frontal lobes, information gathers and is analyzed. It is here the brain makes sense of experiences old and new and plans action. Once Alzheimer's spreads to the front lobes, the chain of actions is no longer guided by an ability to reason.

The final stage of the disease brings a total dependence. Changes in motor abilities affect balance in walking, with the person generally confined to a wheelchair, a geriatric chair, and then a bed. Verbal languages disappear, although non-verbal communication, the reaction to touch or tone of voice, remains present for a long time. The patient has trouble swallowing and chokes while drinking and eating, which leads to aspiration pneumonia, the usual cause of death, occurring eight to ten years after stage 3.

A cure is not yet on the horizon. In a world of increasing numbers of survivors of cancer, major heart attacks, and stroke, there is not a single living survivor of Alzheimer's. What is far more likely than a specific cure is the gradual development and deployment of drugs or other remedies to delay the progression of the disease, reducing the intensity of the suffering it prompts. However, much attention and underwriting may be focused on the laboratory, the battle for life that is Alzheimer's will be principally fought by those who are not physicians or researchers, but by those who are family to the victims and to the caregivers. If the choices we make can delay the progression by five years, we could reduce the incidence of Alzheimer's Disease by 50%, all of it from the latter stages of the disease. Today, a study of biomarkers, new blood tests and scans for Acalaid deposits can provide even earlier warnings.

The work shift in this literally thankless job lasts twenty-four hours a day, seven days a week. Caregivers must be able to diagnose a wide variety of ordinary ailments. Imagine a patient suddenly upset about something, but completely unable to communicate the problem, or even to understand it himself. Is pain real or imagined? Is he hungry? Exhausted? Sore? Is his back in spasm or is his appendix inflamed? Can he point to the problem? No, he cannot.

At Dr. Pugar's suggestion, Mother did have an M.R.I. and the scan, done on an open machine because of Mother's claustrophobia, showed brain shrinkage with a pronounced space between the brain tissue and the skull that is characteristic of Alzheimer's patients. When she did die, there was no proposal for an autopsy, and so one was not performed; but as a matter of record, the family would not have objected.

CHAPTER 13
The Caregivers

Two women came as Mother's first caregivers, and they remained for the entire course of Mother's Alzheimer's illness. Like others who also joined the team as more help was needed, these caring, gifted people became like family.

Missy graduated high school in Happy, Texas, not far from Amarillo and invested two months in obtaining status as a Certified Nursing Assistant, the entry-level qualification required of those who wished to work in a nursing home, hospital, or private setting. Two months' training was hardly excessive. Missy says that Texas then required a longer course of study for beauticians than for those who would care for the elderly, and the responsibility of a Certified Nursing Assistant exceeds what one might expect from an entry level post. "You don't just tie a patient's shoes or help them bathe, but also give medications and injections." She said, "You can drop them, you can give them the wrong medications, you can kill someone." She passed the required written test with ease. During the clinical portion of her qualifying, however, her reviewer had one cause for complaint. Missy, she said, spent too much time washing her hands.

Too much time. Working in a thirty-bed facility near Amarillo and placed in charge of eighteen patients, Missy, then thirty-one, realized that time was simply insufficient. One had to keep moving. Most patients were there because their families had exhausted their capability to provide care in the home. Some patients needed only limited attention. Others could not roll over in bed without assistance, such repositioning was necessary to prevent bedsores. Missy recalled, "I soon learned that that is how nursing homes work. You never have enough time." The work was not particularly remunerative, a fact that lends itself to absenteeism. When needed, Missy worked double shifts and then slept in her car in the parking lot so she could be ready for her next scheduled shift.

Working with patients, Missy learned there was no point in arguing. If the patient said the cat was purple, then the cat was purple. Maybe the patient was referring to something other than the cat. Maybe the patient sincerely thought the cat was purple. Maybe the cat was purple. Missy also learned the characteristic signs of impending death. There would be increased depression and decreased intake of food and beverage. The patient, commonly, would announce they were packing for a trip. They would become preoccupied with packing. Did you remember this? Did you remember that? Did you tell my family? No destination for the trip was ever articulated. Packing for the trip meant readying oneself for death. Missy commented, "I don't think anybody should ever die alone. There should be love and comfort until the final breath. Sensory input is the last connection they lose, they can hear you until the end."

An agency that places caregivers put us in contact with Missy and later with Wanda. Mother and Dad were then on the family boat in Florida, so the Crown Human Resources staff conducted the interview and Missy was offered the job. More specifically, in January 2007 she went to Florida to join Mother and Dad aboard the boat.

Missy's assessment of her new charge was that Mother was in a state of moderately advanced Alzheimer's. She could complete her morning routine, provided she was given directions step-by-step, rather than rattled off in a series. Mother could walk, provided someone held her hand for reassurance, guidance, and support. She could feed herself—"Here's your lunch. Here's your spoon." She recognized most of those around her, and she managed a goodly amount of responsive conversation. Mother did not refer to Missy by name, but called her "my girl." Clearly, Mother really liked Missy.

At this point, Missy also assessed the family. We knew enough already to understand the current staff was not going to be sufficient. We needed people who knew more about dealing with Alzheimer's. We also knew Mother's lifestyle was going to require change. Mother was someone who had never preferred showers, but she had not had a full bath in a tub in nearly two years. If presented with a bathtub, she would scream.

Commonly, Alzheimer patients combine a fear of the act of bathing with a deep discomfort at being wet. The fear goes beyond bathing to a fear of water itself. Externally, an Alzheimer's patient may seem indifferent, and appear to be living in their own inner world. Reactions, however, to sensory stimuli become more acute. What the average person might regard as a tolerably damp shirt is simple intolerably soggy to an Alzheimer's sufferer. Sense impressions need to be moderated. Sunglasses are worn to blunt the light of day. Mother favored embroidered blouses. With time, the threads on the inside of the blouses became an irritant that she rejected. "I don't want that. It's scratchy," she would say. As the mind loses the power to rationalize reality, feeling comes to the fore.

Dad held to the belief that Mother could master most of the problems she faced, simply by demonstrating more determination. In the early days on the boat, Dad felt Missy's central task was to press Mother to make a greater effort. Missy's view was that she was there to give her patient all needed assistance. On one occasion, Mother was in the bathroom talking to herself. Dad told Missy to wait outside. Missy sensed that while Mother wanted her help, she could not remember how to summon her. "So, I went in and closed the door. I figured if he fired me, he fired me, but she was the person who needed help."

Dad thought such behavior constituted coddling. At one point, he gave Missy a verbal "correction" that nearly reduced her to tears.

After Missy left the room, Captain Mike confronted Dad. Mike said, "You understand, don't you, that if you lose Missy, Eilleen can't be on the boat anymore, which means you won't be on the boat anymore." Dad was a strong personality, but he handled pushback well. Mike was not a "yes" man and when he pushed, Dad listened. "Well," he told Mike, "I guess I'd better apologize."

At the same time, Mother maintained a sense of her independence. At one point on the boat, Missy recollects it as June 2007, my 86-year-old mother took exception to something Dad had said.

Pointing a finger in his direction, she said, "Jim Dicke, you can be replaced."

To which her husband of over sixty-five years replied mildly, "Oh, Eilleen."

Some months after Missy's arrival, she was joined by a second professional caregiver, Wanda. Wanda was born and raised in Jamestown, Pennsylvania, a dot of a place sixty miles north of Pittsburgh. As the oldest of five children whose parents worked shifts, Wanda was from the age of nine or ten often left in charge of the younger ones. She said she always had the caring spirit, and the neighborliness common to small towns. If the neighbors had a new baby, for example, people simply went over and helped out as needed.

After high school, Wanda was married for thirty-one years to a local dairy farmer, a union that produced the four children she regards as her life's greatest accomplishment. Following a divorce, Wanda's still "caring spirit" took her into nursing. Hospital or institutional nursing jobs held no appeal. She wanted to work with a family, preferably one not too far from her children in Pennsylvania. When the placement agency matched her with Mother and Dad in neighboring Ohio, she took the job, originally sharing an apartment with Missy in the family guesthouse. As Wanda came, it was also becoming clear that Mother and Dad could no longer be on the boat.

Mother was just moving into the later stages of Alzheimer's. She was, Wanda said, "Just a grand, classy, wonderful person with a great sense of humor."

> "She could walk if someone supported an arm. We had to dress her, and she always wanted nice dressy clothes and jewelry and pretty shoes. She was accustomed to dressing like that. She was eighty-five when I started. She would have her hair beautifully done and she always wanted to wear a ball cap. A baseball-style cap, but not necessarily one with a logo. She would wear them every day, even around the house."

Mother was not housebound. Wanda remembers in the earlier days, "We would all go to Indian Lake for lunch. Those were fun times. She enjoyed getting dressed up for dinner, and appreciated favorite jokes."

As time passed, conversation focused increasingly on family—her parents, her sisters, and her sons. Wanda observed, "Up until she died, her family is what she enjoyed talking about." She also talked about pets they had owned, particularly a Great Dane named Duke. Duke was so well trained that when he came into the house, he would clean his feet in a tray of water left just inside the door. Prompted, Mother's memory would extend itself. She would recall trips on the boat, its captain, Mike, and the crew by name, along with numerous memories of David and Ruth Ann.

Originally, Wanda thought it would be a two-year assignment. Then it overran her expectations. While some later caregivers moved on, finding the work too repetitive, Wanda stayed longer than intended, a commonality she shared with Missy. Despite Mother's infirmities, and despite her occasional threats to "throw you in the pond" or "hit you with a hammer," Wanda viewed Mother "as such a blessing to me, and to a lot of the caregivers. She always gave back to me more than I gave her. We would have girl parties. We'd tell her, 'We're going to have a party at your house because we can eat and drink and dance and sing at your house,' and she just loved that." "Eilleen," Wanda recalled, "would always say to us, 'Don't you worry, honey. I'll take good care of you.' She enjoyed talking to the girls about their husbands and children. Conversation did not always have to be about her."

With Alzheimer's, the brain dies in predictable stages. Commonly, the longest and strongest held memories are musical, particularly the memories of songs one took to heart in late adolescence and early adulthood. Some important studies have been done about the therapeutic benefits of music and singing with Alzheimer's patients. "I had one patient who was completely non-responsive," neurologist Dr. Pugar said, "but when he heard Count Basie, he lit up like a light bulb. For another, it was Jimi Hendrix." When Wanda arrived, Mother still had a powerful sweet singing voice. Wanda recalled, "We'd say, 'Eilleen, let's do the hoochie-coochie.' And she would move her hips in time with that." She liked Frank Sinatra and Dean Martin. She was partial to "Love Letters in the Sand" and "Tea for Two." But there was no question of what song headed her personal top-of-the-charts. For Mother, nothing beat "Show Me the Way to Go Home." Professors at the University of Dayton suggested introducing music more pervasively in Mother's daily routine and they were right. It was a major help.

CHAPTER 14

When All Else Fails

Mother and Dad were people who lead adult lives centered on family, friends, work and travel. Over the years, they declined most opportunities for board involvements, with a few notable exceptions. They especially enjoyed their experiences, educational opportunities, and friendships that came with their membership in the Young Presidents' Organization. Especially for a family trying to develop a family business in a rural community, YPO offered the chance of friendships and business idea exchange with other families who had similar interests and challenges. Dad and Mother fit in with and enjoyed being a part of a community, whether it was New Bremen, YPO, Culver, or Ocean Reef. They were not people who made the effort to attend galas. They were not big party givers, for the most part, or big party attendees. At various times in their lives, they might enjoy an evening meal with the same good friend several nights in a row and even enjoy going to the same restaurant night after night. Therefore, later, as Mother began to develop memory issues, it did not seem unusual when they would go to the same restaurant night after night, sit at the same table with the same waitress night after night, and even order the same food choices night after night. Whether conscious or unconscious, this became a coping mechanism they both could use to make things all right for one more day, even for one more week, or month, or year.

From the day of their marriage, Mother focused on being a supportive wife, always there for her husband. She followed him to war. They did not adopt hobbies that did not include the other. They fit well together, enhancing the strength of each other's personalities and easing the challenges of each other's shortcomings. Well before Mother was diagnosed, Dad went into the Kettering hospital for a hip replacement. The wrong ball and socket was chosen, and two weeks later they were back switching the wrong hip joint choice for another. We teased Dad that he had initially been given a businessman's hip in error, when what he really needed was a farmer's hip. Dad's reaction was to send his surgeon a case of his favorite wine, to show there were no hard feelings. Both times while he was hospitalized, Mother slept in the hospital also and would not leave his side. It was a choice she made for her own comfort, in addition to being supportive of Dad. It is said, no one knows anything about anyone's marriage except their own and they only know about 50% of that one. With that in mind, let me offer a few observations on what their relationship looked like to me.

They were very devoted to one another, to the exclusion of all else. All other relationships, family, professional, friends or otherwise served to take a back seat to their devotion to one another. Mother was meticulous. She was deliberate. Dad was always nudging her to move a bit faster. If she was chronically late and Dad started suggesting earlier departure times so they would be on time, she would see through the ploy, challenge his calculation, and when all else failed, just ignore. Yet, unfailingly, they never suggested going to an event separately and meeting there. It would have never have occurred to either of them. Each evening, Dad would be ready to go to bed before Mother, yet he always insisted that he would not go to sleep until she had come to bed. Dad would sit in bed, propped up with a pillow, watching Johnny Carson, until Mother came to bed. The pattern may have come from both of their parents. A pattern of the husband as provider and protector, and the wife as the one who ruled the roost was the norm in both the family homes in which they had been raised. Having gotten through those early years when Dad traveled a lot for business, they reached a stage where they no longer needed to be apart for the needs of the business, and so they would not. There seemed to be a moment in the early 1950s when an abrupt transition happened. Dad was on a business trip in New York when, as a passenger in a car, he was injured in an auto accident that left him with a scar on his cheek. Dad called Mother to tell her what had happened and that he was fine. He flew home, and when he got off the plane and Mother saw his face half bandaged, she started weeping uncontrollably. After that, Dad made almost no solo business trips.

They say stress and unhappiness are not good for Alzheimer's patients. The best strategy is to have each day be a good day. Don't argue. For Mother and Dad, the bulwark of contentment was what they found with each other. Stress came when they saw family and friends needing to deal with troublesome situations, but they did not have stress with each other. A perceptive young Jim III would say "Gram is a worrier" and he was right. She could be deeply distressed over any illness or hurt that impacted family or friends. She could be especially emotional, if she thought she was being blamed for something. Dad was always firmly protective. His never-failing efforts for her contentment was the best possible medicine.

In the 1980s, Mother's two daughters-in-law, Janet and Kerry, decided that it would be fun to have a week-long girls' excursion to the "Greenhouse," an upscale lady's spa, and exercise experience in Dallas. Mother thought it was a wonderful opportunity to be with her daughters-in-law. She was particularly pleased they would want her to join them for the week. On reflection, however, she extracted a condition. Mother would go to the spa for a week, only if her two sons would go somewhere with their father for the week so he would not be alone. It was a very Eilleen-like "condition."

When I was a child, after John Glenn orbited the earth, Mother spoke often about wanting to go to the moon, to go everywhere, and to see everything. She never heard of a place that she would not want to see, and, once there, everywhere was a place where she intended to return one day. However, on a trip to Moscow in the 1960s when she was in her 40s, Mother developed a life-long case of claustrophobia, triggered when she and Dad were trapped in a hotel elevator with a number of people for several hours. As she got older, her claustrophobia became more pronounced. After the Russian elevator incident, I never again heard her talk of a moon trip. She developed an aversion to being in small planes. Any situation where she thought she could be trapped brought on symptoms of panic. This was almost three decades before any onset of her dementia.

As Mother's dementia became pronounced, her attorneys thought it would be prudent for Mother to appoint a power of attorney. Her granddaughter Jennifer would agree to serve. Mother was so much in denial about her memory problems that there was some doubt in my mind that Mother would actually sign. On the appointed day, however, Grandpa Webster's good business-minded daughter handled the matter like a professional. Mother expressed confidence in her granddaughter, asked the attorney if the document was ok to sign, asked me to assure her that this was just a precautionary matter and that I did not yet think it was needed, and then with handwriting that showed her infirmity, while Dad sat silently, she signed. Thankfully, it was indeed precautionary. Jennifer never had to exercise the authority granted from her grandmother, but the incident illustrated how Mother could still summon the elements and decision-making process of a business question.

One day, as Mother was being wheeled to the south end of the house for her shower, she was complaining loudly that the nurses were torturing her and that she would get them, when she noticed she was being wheeled past her husband. She paused for a second, loudly proclaimed, "Not you, Jim, you're okay," and then immediately went back to her protest. Everyone had a good laugh. It is easy for the observer of the Alzheimer's sufferer to draw an incorrect conclusion. Words that are used may have no connection to thoughts. Phrases are uttered that may have no connection whatsoever to anything really at hand. Yet, if there was a constant to Mother's days, it was that she never seemed to lose track of who Dad was. Other family and loved ones might seem confusing or indistinct, but "my husband Jim" was always "okay."

It is difficult to know what might be a significant early warning of Alzheimer's and what is not. Some years ago, a friend had a brain operation and developed a nose drip that would not go away, which ultimately was identified as a slow drip of brain fluid into her nasal cavity. It made me think of Mother. For decades, Mother carried little packages of tissues in her purse or pocket, and she almost continually had a little tissue in her hand. Both she and Dad were fundamentally healthy people, but all day, every day she would blow and dab with the ever-present tissue.

Missy said, "When I first met Eilleen, she would never leave her dressing room in the morning unless both pockets of her shorts contained a packet of folded tissues. Eilleen lovingly referred to these as 'my nose blowers.' One summer afternoon in New Bremen while I was sitting at the kitchen table with Eilleen and Jim, she leaned over to me after blowing her nose and said to Missy with a smile, 'When all else fails, blow your nose.' Then she laughed. As the years passed, she could no longer find them in her pocket. The caregivers would have them folded and in sight for her, and she would ask for them as well. Then the time came when she would forget to take them or ask, so the caregivers would just hand them to her. Sometimes Mother would just use her blanket, as it was close to her face, so they would assist. She never lost the will or desire or ability to wipe her nose, not until hospice care started.

As the Alzheimer's took its toll, each time I visited, I would make a point of addressing her as Mother and tell her I loved her. She would sit silently, staring, but you could read volumes in those brown eyes. On one hand, she was not quite sure who I was, but she could tell I looked familiar. Probably I was family? She was sure I was not her husband, but not so sure if I was a brother or a son or, if so, which one. Mother would play it safe and not respond at all. She was not overly curious to solve the riddle, did not want to admit confusion, and I had no appetite for trying to pull a response. At least this is what I thought I saw. Neither Grandma Dicke nor Grandma Webster had ever given me biting or cruel comments in their times of dementia. The same can be said for my mother, but I also never pushed my luck.

CHAPTER 15

More Caregivers Come

Following the hiring of Missy and Wanda, the caregiving team expanded. This followed two decisions. First, we recognized care for Mother was needed 24/7. Second, we realized an extension of care was needed for Dad, who, while not suffering from Alzheimer's, was declining with age. Over time, the caregiving staff grew to about a dozen.

The neurologist, Dr. Kenneth Pugar, was mildly in awe of them.

> "Whether her caregivers were devoutly religious or not, they had the sense that they were doing God's good work. I notice that same thing in the good nursing home workers. They have that same smile on their face, whether they're cleaning feces off of someone, or dealing with other unpleasant things. How does someone find that rewarding? Somehow they do."

Further, Dr. Pugar was impressed with the consequences of their efforts. "Eilleen's skin was soft as a 40-year old's, because of all the massage and the oils. She never had bedsores. She never had what I call that 'old age smell.' She always had her hair and nails in good shape."

Some caregivers were recruited from Crown's existing employees. That selecting was generally done by Crown's personnel department and Kathy, one of the Crown executives who focuses on special projects. Some of those hired had caregiving in their backgrounds, others had never considered the possibility. All went through a series of interviews. Kathy said, "We would ask them point blank about personal care. Did they really know what was involved? Could they be okay with that?" Selections reflected a combination of information and intuition. The intent was to identify people with caregiver skills, who could work as a team, and who would respect the confidentiality of the family. To provide round-the-clock coverage for both Mother and Dad, caregivers alternated weeks of three and four twelve-hour shifts. Kathy commented, "I don't think I could ever find a better group of people. They were great." The goal was to always have someone at hand to be helpful to Mother and Dad all day, every day. The caregivers became a part of the extended family. In later stages, it could require two or three or even four caregivers to re-position or help with basic necessities. It was a very people-intensive hands-on challenge. Dr. David Imler and Dr. David Louis provided the regular medical oversight.

Considered as a group, some common themes emerge. Most strikingly, virtually all the caregivers had been middle children. A goodly number during their high school years had cared for an aging relative and found the experience rewarding.

Dani started on the day of Mother's weekly shower. Mother hated getting wet. She also hated anything sharp, so the women giving her the sponge bath in the shower room would make sure their fingernails were filed and all rings were removed. Nonetheless, Mother made her displeasure known. Dani said, "She would curse and say, 'I'm going to get a hammer and kill you,' or 'I'm going to throw you in the damn pond.' So, we got Eilleen in the shower and I looked her in the eye and she said, 'Damn it, you got me all wet.' I looked at her and said, 'You got me all wet, too.' She said, 'You think you're so goddamned smart.' Then we both laughed."

Wendy, who started working with Mother in 2013, recalls her first-day nervousness. That day, Mother was having a very good day. Wendy recalled, "I remember when they brought me in and introduced me to her, she kept saying, 'Don't you worry; we'll take good care of you.' Over and over. I learned later that was just something she said when she was having a good day, but at the time it made me feel very welcome."

Carolyn said, "Everyone loved Eilleen and her sweetness. She would tell you stories about her life. She was just funny and she liked to have a good time." The caregivers' sense of community grew. One caregiver recalled being invited to put pictures of her own children on the piano. Dani recalled realizing that no permission was required to help herself to a Coke from the refrigerator. Further, Kevin noted there was a clear policy that the caregiver's own family needs came first. If he needed time off to attend a child's conference at school, or a daughter's dance recital, or to take his children trick-or-treating, accommodations were made that might not have been likely in an institutional setting. Dad routinely inquired about the caregivers' lives. If one said her son was about to head off for two weeks at Boy Scout camp, then two weeks later he would raise the subject and ask how the time had been enjoyed.

Dani said, "I had to work a lot of Thanksgivings, Christmases, and New Year's. This was the first time in my life that I never dreaded coming to work, because I felt like this was my second home and my second family." Obviously, close physical care for ailing individuals includes much that many would find unpleasant to do. Dan, however, probably spoke for others as well when he said, "The toughest part of the job was watching them both deteriorate."

CHAPTER 16

No Survivors

Human beings can survive a great deal—from plane crashes, to earthquakes, to combat wounds, to cancer—but there are, to date, no survivors of Alzheimer's disease.

This fact is central to the treatment of Alzheimer's patients. One truism among those performing Alzheimer's care is to avoid long-term thinking. Because the long-term reality is that the sufferer is going to become less and less able, less and less responsive, less and less present, and then the sufferer is going to die. Proper emphasis, therefore, is placed on the here and now, on trying to make any given day a good day, on maintaining as much as one can of the patient's web of human interactions.

When Missy and Wanda started working with Mother in 2007, she was, in Wanda's words, "very ambulatory. All you had to do is hold her by the tips of the fingers and just guide her along. She just walked very well by herself. She could pace really quickly; particularly if she was a little upset." At that time, Mother still ate solid foods. Her favorites were banana nut mini-muffins, which were soft, moist. She once ate eighteen at a single sitting. She also favored banana cream pie, which became banana cream pudding when she stopped eating the crust. She liked chicken. She liked shrimp. Mother was allergic to garlic, and so that was something to be avoided. Garlic would trigger gastric pain upset, diarrhea, and sometimes even fever. After banana cream pudding, her favorite desert became ice cream with a cookie. Missy commented, "A trick I learned over the years was that if you can't get an older patient to eat, sprinkle it with sugar or salt." With age, the taste buds lose sensitivity. Food becomes unappetizing, because it ceases to taste of much, and so extra salt and sugar bring the appetite back. Mother, for example, maintained a fondness for potato chips and chocolate chip cookies.

I recall having three very difficult age-related conversations with Dad. The first involved securing Dad's agreement to surrender his driver's license. The second, about the time of Mother's Alzheimer's diagnosis, was gaining Dad's agreement that their traveling days were over. Mother could no longer manage the disorientating effects of moving from location to location. After that, Mother spent the bulk of her time in the New Bremen family home, where she continued to share a room with Dad. When Wanda first arrived to work with Mother in 2007, she recalled, "They were together all the time. They would wake up in the morning. They would have breakfast together. They would then get dressed and later they would have lunch together." Dad's presence steadied Mother. Once, when Dad had hip surgery, the two were separated overnight so he could sleep undisturbed. Wanda recalled, "She didn't understand why she could not be with him, even though she was in an adjoining room."

My third difficult conversation with Dad came when it was clear that he and Mother could no longer share a bedroom.

Thereafter, Mother spent much of her time in what had been their master bedroom, but became her own suite, with a hospital bed, a recliner, and a portable commode. Mother had a big screen television and her favorites were DVD's of The Lucy Show, occasionally The Carol Burnett Show, and videos made by various members of the family. She was especially pleased by anything having to do with babies. Big pictures of each of her great grandchildren were placed on the wall. She would repeat, "Oh, there are my babies; my babies are so cute."

One aspect of care is working to maintain a daily routine for a patient who, progressively, loses track of the distinctions of day and time. Medications are part of that routine. In 2009, Mother received standard morning dosages of Depakote (to prevent migraines and possible seizures) and Dyazide capsule (diuretic that also guarded against falling potassium levels), along with baby aspirin and vitamins. Depakote repeated at 4 p.m. Her evening meds included Seroquel (which helps balance neurotransmitters in the brain), Ambien, to promote sleep, and 100 mg. of Neurontin (used to treat nerve pain).

The daytime emphasis was on social interaction. Wanda said, "Generally, we would just strike up a conversation. We'd say, 'Well, Eilleen, what do you want to do today? Do you want to go shopping? What do you want to buy? Shall we have lunch out? Let's go get our hair done.' It was that kind of chitter chatter that would get things started. We could ask her all kinds of questions, and she would always answer. And then maybe we would say, 'Well, what are you thinking about, Eilleen?' And she'd always say, 'Where's Jim? Where's Jim Dicke?' We would say, 'Well, he was taking a nap or he was out watching television.' Then she'd want to talk about her family in Dayton, her twin sisters, then reminisce about Jim and their times together. Those were the kinds of things she liked talking about the most."

Mother's nature itself may have helped ease the challenges of the disease. Inexplicable as it may seem, virtually all of Mother's caregivers volunteered the statement that they felt they received back from Mother more than they were providing with their care. Wanda said, "She was such a blessing to me, and to a lot of the caregivers. She was so kind and appreciative of us. In early years, she was just a joy to take care of."

Mother would tell stories for the caregivers, about things that went on, about where she had lived, and people she had known. She liked to joke about a dishonest boat captain she had met who would say, "You can trust me." She thought if someone had to say, "You can trust me," they probably were not trustworthy. So, the caregivers would say, "Trust me," and that would make her laugh. She remembered, in the beginning.

As a somewhat distant second to bathing, Carolyn recalled, "She hated going to the toilet." The urge to go was accompanied by complaints about Frances. "She said it a million times," said Carolyn. "'That old Frances,' she would just say. No one knew who her imaginary Frances was." A second caregiver recalled, "A lot of times she would say, 'Get him out of here; I don't want him here,' but there was no 'him' present. Often, we told her we had had 'Molly,' the nickname of a former New Bremen policeman whose name Eilleen recalled, come take whoever it was away. And she would say, 'Oh, okay.' It was kind a comical, though we never laughed. The solution was a matter of redirecting her attention."

As time passed, Mother needed support from each side to walk. Gradually, walking became beyond her capability. Three people were required, one on each side, a third maneuvering the chair, to move her from her bed to her beside commode, her recliner, or her wheelchair.

Alzheimer's progressively attacks different areas of the brain. Hostile eruptions and bursts of anxiety may occur all out of proportion to events, or even for no discernable reason. For Mother, such outbursts started in mid-2010, when the daily nursing notes begin to record abrupt swings from good cheer to threatening bad temper. A sampling of extracts follows:

July 5, 2010:

7:15 pm – Keeps looking at birthday flowers and stating, "Aren't they beautiful." "Don't you think they're beautiful?"

8:15 pm – Started yelling get her out of here.

8:30 pm – "Get me out of here. She's killing me."

July 7, 2010:

11:30 am – Talked, screamed, hit the bed. Mood fluctuating from one minute to next.

3:42 pm – Eilleen has been so pleasant this afternoon. Very social and pleasant.

July 8, 2010:

8:30 pm – Up to bathroom. Screaming, cussing, combative.

July 9, 2010:

7:00 pm – Singing and then yelling "get her out of here" and then back to singing, sipping on Ensure & listening to music & then singing & back to yelling "get her out of here."

7:30 pm – "Tennessee Waltz" came on and she calmed down and was pleasant. Sipping on Ensure, watching Lucy.

July 11, 2010:

5:50 am – Bathroom trip. Hitting and cursing staff.

6:15 am – In recliner yelling & hitting staff. Ativan given in side of cheek. Ativan given with Ensure. 100% taken. Listening to music. Still yelling & hitting staff. There are periods when she is quiet and then bursts out in yelling & pulling on staff clothes.

7:05 pm – Grabbed my hand with meds & Ensure cup in hand and she started hitting Ensure & meds all over floor and me. Cleaned up. Watching video of family, still saying, "Get me out of here." Music playing, calm & then burst of yelling & hissing.

8:00 pm – Eilleen still agitated. "It is absolute murder."

11:00 pm – In bed, yelling, "I hate you!" Asleep within 10 mins.

The elderly can be capable of considerable resistance. Wanda said, "When she would get upset with you, when there was something you wanted her to do that she didn't want to do, she was very strong. She'd grab your wrist if you were trying to feed her; and she had a very firm grip when she was upset. The outbursts came when you were trying to move her or dress her. She just didn't want you to touch her. She would scream at us; she would call us names. Mainly, the outbursts happened when she didn't want to eat."

As confusion advances, Alzheimer's patients characteristically go through a period of resistance, often physically expressed.

Compared to the average sufferer, Mother's periods of determined resistance were brief. Caregiver Ali recalled, "She wasn't cranky for a length of time, probably never more than a half-hour or hour of carrying on and yelling out."

Mother's difficult period roughly corresponded with a 2010 visit that I paid to Dr. Kenneth Pugar, at the neurologist's invitation. I approached the meeting with misgivings, concerned that Dr. Pugar was going to suggest moving Mother to a facility near Dayton, which, if recommended, I thought the family should resist. At the meeting, Dr. Pugar said some hard decisions needed to be made. For example, if Mother no longer wished to eat, should a feeding tube be introduced? He, the neurologist, recommended against it, but said it was a family decision. The family was clear. Beyond pain medication or any steps that would normally be taken, no extraordinary means were to be used to keep Mother alive. At meeting's end, I said I was relieved that this was the conversation we had, because I thought we were going to talk about Mother moving into a senior care facility. It was a relief when Dr. Pugar said, "People in professional facilities can't get the level of care she is getting at home. Keep her there."

We tried to be forthcoming with whatever the caregivers thought was needed. Rachel said, "Jim II made it easy for us, because any time we had a new idea or needed a new product or we said we needed fifteen of something, we would just tell Jim II and it would come. If we needed a certain wheelchair, we got the wheelchair."

Technology, however, was less important than human skill. For example, when Mother was distressed, one standard approach was redirection—simply changing the subject. Sometimes, caregivers would ask about Eddie Steppe, a boy pal from Mother's childhood years. "She'd just light up. And the caregivers would tease her... 'Is Eddie Steppe your boyfriend?' She would say 'Yes.' And she would smile." Actually, Eddie Steppe was a friend of Mother and Dad's from their Stivers High School days, but also someone who had been in Mother's school class since kindergarten. The last time I saw Eddie Steppe was at Grandpa Webster's visitation at the funeral home in Dayton. Eddie had become a public city bus driver. He left his city bus, with passengers, parked by the side of the road in front of the funeral home saying, "I'll be right back," and came into the funeral home to pay Mr. Webster his last respects. The retelling of Eddie doing that always gave everyone a good chuckle.

When Mother experienced pain, the caregivers' first attempt would be to talk her through it, perhaps by redirection. In an institutional setting, by contrast, a patient in pain is likely to be medicated. While medication may manage the moment, its long-term use hastens the decline in acuity.

Besides redirection, there was indirection. Once bedridden, it was important for Mother to have her arms and legs massaged frequently to prevent edema (the buildup of liquid in the extremities). Missy recalled, "She wasn't going to do anything Jim wouldn't do. As a new person, I had to gently work with Jim, for him to understand the massage was something we really had to do. We had to get her permission before we could touch Jim's feet. We would say, 'Can we give Jim a foot message?' And she'd say, 'Honey, do you want a foot massage?' He would say, 'Yes.' And then she would say, 'OK.' Jim would then say, 'Would you like to have one?' That's how it became part of her routine." Another caregiver noted, "Sometimes her ankles would swell; the next day maybe she'd be back to normal again. Her knees often hurt, she would sit with one foot turned out to be more comfortable." The effects of massage pleased Dr. Pugar. To the end, he said, she was entirely without blemish or skin problems.

Among other activities, Mother enjoyed mentally mapping her family tree. A caregiver said, "We would always say that we were with her. Dorothy and Doris [her sisters] and her mother were there, and her father was there. She didn't know that they weren't there, because we were giving them to her. We would talk about her wedding to Jim, and how it had taken place in the morning because Jim's cousin Lucille was getting married that same afternoon. We would remind her of those things."

Wanda noted, "Eilleen would relate to the male caregivers. There would be some days when she would tune us out; but, when male caregivers who were taking care of Jim would come back to her bedroom, instantly, Eilleen would perk right up—smile, laugh and joke. The male caregivers would play up to her, saying things like 'Eilleen, you look beautiful today. You look lovely.' She would say, 'Thank you.'" Kevin, one of those called upon, said, "I'd sit with her and hold her hand. She knew when you were trying to put one over on her, like when you would tell her meds were a Yellowbird, which is an island's rum drink. She just looked at me and said, 'Oh, bull.' She was no dummy."

The most common approach to Mother's comfort involved music. This is generally true with Alzheimer's patients. My brother Dane recalls that, when visiting, "I used to like to sing with her. She would know who I was. The caregivers would help her with the names. 'Dane's here.' I would say, 'Why don't we sing a song?' And the suggestion would be, "Mares Eat Oats and Does Eat Oats" or "An Irish Lullaby."

Mother's strongest support was Dad. Though his own health was not good, he remained kind and always put her needs first. He was unpretentious and Dad was, in all things but politics, a democrat. The first week after Carol began as their housekeeper, she learned that Dad liked cole slaw and set out to make a batch. Carol recalled, "I had to cut this head of cabbage. I tell you, I had slaw all over the place. He came in the house, took his tie off, rolled up his sleeves, and said, 'Let me show you, Carol, how to cut cabbage.' And he did." They were very good people to work for. She had me put my family pictures on the piano, and said I should feel like I was at home."

That graciousness even continued as Dad neared his own final days in November 2016. Weekly, he still had his hair and nails done by the ladies who had done the same chores for Mother for years. Dad always made small talk. Julie F., their longtime hairdresser, recalls, "I was eating powdered peanut butter for protein. He wanted to know where to get some." He always asked if they had received "their envelopes" with their compensation, and each week always gave each a small gift, say, a Crown company pen, though with the admonition, "Don't tell Eilleen about this."

Dad was all but utterly uncritical of Mother. Caregiver Dani recalled, "I don't remember him ever saying one bad word about Eilleen. In most marriages, people will say a thing, jokingly, about their spouse. Jim would say, 'There's nothing bad to be said; she's a wonderful woman. I don't think we ever had an argument.'" When my brother Dane demurred, "Dad, I think Mother let you know how it was going to be a couple of times," Dad replied, "We always discussed things and we never went to bed angry." As Mother's condition deteriorated, they spent less time together. One caregiver stated, "When she would have outbursts or get agitated, it was hard for Jim to watch the way she was. We kept them separated a bit more." Dani recalled, "The minute she would hear his voice, she would perk up and look in his eyes and call him her bulldog. He would always growl for her and tell her that he loved her." The bulldog reference must have been something of a private joke between them. While researching for this book, I could find no school that either one of them had ever been associated with, where the school mascot was a bulldog. Yet, throughout life, Mother would occasionally announce as we were about to leave for somewhere, "Here we go bulldogs!"

Truth be told, Mother enjoyed the attention of the male caregivers. Her failing health required the men's help to move her from bed to recliner. The men included Kevin and Dan. The women's caregivers would tell Mother when Dan was present, and she knew who they were talking about. Dan remembered, "I was 'Dan, the Muffin Man.' They would give me a muffin and I would feed it to her." Whenever the men were needed to help with Mother, Dad directed they do so immediately. One caregiver recalled, "It didn't matter what they were in the middle of, it might be breakfast or lunch. If we were needed to move Eilleen, he would say, 'Take your time; whatever Eilleen needs.'"

Mother may have been a bit of a flirt herself, but she could be jealous of the women caregivers. She would say she could take care of Dad, and they didn't need to hover over him. On one occasion, shortly after surgery had left Dad encumbered with a catheter, Missy, needing to change the bag, got down near Dad's knees, and Mother said, "Are you having fun down there?" and casually kicked Missy on her backside.

A further aspect of Alzheimer's care is to promote the patient's ties with the broader web of human interactions. Kevin's daughter was born in October 2010, two months after he started working with Mother and Dad. His son was born not quite three years later. Kevin said, "I took the kids to see Eilleen, because she loved babies. She just loved babies." Rachel started in 2012. "When I got hired, we had glimpses of what Eilleen was like. Being one of the youngest caregivers there, I think she saw a bit of herself in me. I wore my hair down, like she had. The other caregivers would call me her 'baby doll.' They'd say, 'Your baby doll is here today,' and Eilleen would just look at me and smile."

As new caregivers came on, one priority was to learn whatever they could of Mother's life story from other caregivers. Rebekkah explained, "When you're dealing with people with Alzheimer's, you really need as much background about them, so you can know what they might be referring to. It's no longer possible for them to tell you those stories themselves." Some behaviors, however, remained inexplicable. This report includes the following:

Tuesday, June 18, 2012:

10:25 am – Grinding teeth hard. Drank most of an Ensure. Went back to grinding teeth.

7:15 pm – Agitating, grinding teeth, refusing to drink.

7:40 pm – Grinding and agitation continues.

9 pm – Still grinding. Have laid her back on recliner and still grinding, will not stop grinding. Music playing.

9:40 pm – Awake drinking. Continues to grind teeth.

The following day was no better.

6:30 am – Eilleen would be quiet and appear to be resting and then start grinding her teeth and hitting the bed.

Nor was June 22

5:45 pm – Starting to grind teeth.

6:30 – 7:00 pm – Very agitated. Grinding LOUDLY. Refusing to drink. Music [Nat King Cole] turned on at 7 pm. Fell asleep within a few minutes. The grinding and agitation continued for weeks to the concern and somewhat to the confusion of the caregivers.

Carolyn recalled, "The teeth grinding would get so bad, we never knew why. All of us together would try to figure out what the problem was. Was she agitated about something? Is it just a mental thing that she doesn't know about? But there would be times when it would be really bad. And then it just went away. Wanda said,

> "We never could figure out what caused the teeth grinding. All twelve of us would talk about it. She wore off a couple of caps from her teeth grinding them so intensely, we found broken off crowns in her mouth. There didn't seem to be anything we could do to help and nothing in particular seemed to start it. She would start grinding on her own and then later just stop on her own. We tried to talk her out of it. We would sing to her, and she would sing with us at some times. At other times, she would just sit there and continue to grind her teeth. When her mind could not get clear on something, that's when the grinding

> would start. Maybe it was a way of trying to put something right."

Wendy suggested the grinding was the result of a confused brain. "I noticed a lot of the teeth grinding happened when she had a red nose or an allergy. She didn't understand to blow her nose. It was like an infant faced with some sort of internal frustration, but not knowing what to do. Sometimes I think she was in pain. I would think at some point the grinding would hurt, but she just kept doing it. It might have been something mentally out of control."

Mother had actually experienced a period earlier in her life where she had ground her teeth in her sleep. Her dentist had installed gold crowns on her molars and the reflex had disappeared; but then with late-stage Alzheimer's, the teeth grinding returned with an ear-splitting persistence. It remained a mystery.

Dr. Pugar said, "Past some point, an Alzheimer's patient does not know how to express themselves. 'I have a headache; I'm dizzy.' They know something is wrong but they don't remember the appropriate behavioral response. These behaviors, wringing the hands, grinding the teeth, saying the same thing over and over, are all fairly common."

And there were certainly times when no one could tell what was wrong. Carolyn said, "Some days, you were at a complete loss. Maybe it was her belly hurting, and you'd get a heating pad and some Miralax." Most commonly, when uncomfortable Mother would just say she wanted to be "nice and dry." This was less a literal statement than Mother's all-purpose phrase for everything being well.

I would come by and tell Mother I loved her, then asking Missy, "Does she even know I am here?" She knew, Missy assured me, but I was not so sure.

Holidays were generally low key. Too many people or too much stimulation could overwhelm both Mother and Dad. Dani recalled of Thanksgiving, "Most of the time, it was just Jim and

Eilleen and the caregivers. Family would call him. The phone would ring all day, but there would be just a very relaxed dinner, nothing elaborate."

In Mother's last few years, the caregivers began narrowing Mother's contacts to close family and friends whose presence would not promote stress. Fewer friends called. Those remembered the best, and longest, were David and Ruth Ann. Ruth Ann recalled, "Towards the end, she still knew who I was. She would respond and smile, but she wouldn't talk. She always knew when I came. She was always the hostess. It was a sad time for me because I thought I had lost such a beautiful friend; she was part of our life." Caregiver Rebekkah said, "It was very obvious that she knew who Ruth Ann was. What I saw in Eilleen was that she still had a gift for conversation. Even to the very end, she would have a conversation about nothing in particular because she couldn't find any words. You might say, 'Oh, it's such a beautiful day,' and she would mumble, but she had the rhythm and the emotion of the conversation correct. I guess that came from years and years of being able to talk to anybody, being able to carry herself in front of the wide range of people with whom she came in contact, so those social graces just remained, even if the language was gone."

The musical connection continued. When, in the last year or two, Mother could no longer remember her children's names, she could remember the words to her songs. Mother had her favorites like "Show Me the Way to Go Home", a song she and the caregivers would sing a dozen times a day.

Missy says, "As things got smaller with her, Eilleen's vocalizing was obsessive and her thoughts focused around her nightgown, babies, being nice and dry, going home, and Jim. When she was verbal, those were the five things she constantly talked about. One day, it occurred to me that a common song everyone knows from childhood and makes them happy is "Happy Birthday to You." So, I took the melody to that song, and I took the topics that she would worry or obsess about—'nice and dry' and 'I want to go home' and

'I want to see Jim'—and I put all those words into that tune and created a song just for her."

Carolyn stated, "As time went on, she had little non-verbal things she would do with us. She was not a touchy-feely hugger, but once she made the motion to touch you, then it was okay to touch her. Our special thing was that she would lean over to let me give her a kiss on the cheek. Once Eilleen liked you, you knew you were okay." Dani recalled, "I could get her to wink. I'd say, 'Eilleen, give me a wink.' And she'd wink and she'd start laughing. That was everybody's joke. I could get Eilleen to wink and to whistle. Eilleen always said two things to me—'You're a hoot" and "You're crazy as a loon.'"

Carolyn added, "Toward the end, we would take her out to see Jim and she would sit with him. They were so sweet with each other. He was very patient with her. There were times we would leave her out there until it was time for her to get ready for bed and change her into her nightgown. We would tell her it's time to go, and give Jim a kiss." Another caregiver recalled, "We would say to her, 'Your husband Jim loves you so much. Do you realize how much he loves you?' And she would say, 'Yes, he's the most kind, caring, wonderful man. You would think he was God.'" She would say that at different times and it just brought down the house.

By this time, Mother's diet had dwindled. Increasingly, she lived on Ensure, a high-protein, high-calorie drink, which, mixed with ice cream, resembled a milkshake. She drank Breeze, a vitamin-enriched beverage a bit thinner than orange juice. These, Wanda said, when mixed with a fortified snack called Magic Cup, produced something like a sherbet. As Mother's appetite declined, the nutritional emphasis shifted to maintaining calorie sufficiency with high-protein, high-calorie drinks.

One way to measure decline is to focus on something simple, like the subject of hair care. This was a matter of some consequence to Mother. Before her illness, housekeeper Carol recalled, she, Mother and Dad went to Dayton every Wednesday to get her hair done. By then, Mother had given in to wearing baseball caps. She had, Carol said, a cap to match every outfit. Carol recalled, "Every time when it was time to leave to get her hair done, Jim would sit out in the car waiting for her. He would wait very patiently for a while, but when he knew they had to be leaving, he would honk for her. She would be at the door, turn around, go back into the bathroom and sit there, just orneriness, because she hated to be rushed."

Mother became a regular customer at "It's All About You", a beauty salon in Ft. Loramie, another Ohio small town nearby. There, for years, they styled Mother's hair, and did pedicure and nails. She was accompanied by two nurses each time, generally Missy, Wanda or Dani. Missy said of the salon, "They knew her. They knew she didn't want to get wet. They did her hair sitting up." Appointments were set for Wednesdays in mid-afternoon, a quiet, generally slack time when perhaps only three of the shop's seven stations would be busy. Dad went too, for his weekly haircut. Mother was generally silent. Dad was all geniality, telling stories and jokes and distributing his characteristic $2 bills to the children of every parent who gave their permission. He was finicky about the haircut itself, always asking someone to check to be sure the part in his hair was straight.

Julia M. of the hair salon stated, "I just recall she always came in wearing a ball cap. She loved to shop, and she would buy pieces of costume jewelry we sell in the salon, which I thought was ironic because she was wearing the real thing." With time, the visits became a problem, both for Mother and for the salon. As Mother's tolerance for multiple places declined, the shop became a threatening place. Mother became difficult to work with, loud and agitated, behavior that children who were in the salon could not understand. Mother stopped asking for her hair to be colored and without discussion, they just stopped the practice. She never noticed, or at least never commented on it, as her hair turned a lovely shade of gray.

With that, Julie F. and Julia M. from the salon started paying visits to Dad and Mother's home. One of the women recalled, "They had a walk-in shower and she would get her hair washed as she was getting her shower. And we would sing to calm her. We would sing: "Show Me the Way to Go Home." She knew the songs, and she sang along. Dad was very attentive. He would ask every day, "How did she do?" Julie F. stated:

> "We had been doing pedicures, but we stopped doing those because her toes were hurting. As far as her nails, I had to be very careful. Sometimes, when she became agitated, she would jerk her hand away and it was possible for her to get a cut. Cleaning under her nails, I had to be very careful. She generally took it OK. Sometimes she would say, 'I'm going to kill you.' She was going to hit us with a hammer. She was strong. I think the first time I got whopped on the head, I just thought, 'Oh my gosh.'"

Julie F. said, "We understood. I can't imagine being in that position and not knowing the people around you. We talked about things. We talked about dancing and going shopping. And then she'd say, 'We don't need anybody. All we need is Jim's credit card. Let's have a girls' night.' After each visit, we took a picture so we could show it to Jim. We'd ask her to wink and tried to capture the 'wink' and smile with a camera."

The Alzheimer's curve is downward, but not uninterruptedly so. The brain of an Alzheimer's sufferer is an almost infinite system of model train tracks that have been so twisted, warped, disconnected, and doubled-back upon themselves that the "trains" carrying whatever message might be intended disappear into gaps, run off the tracks, and are as stymied by blocks as impenetrable as the deep fields of barbed wire that protected the trenches of the First World War. Occasionally, however, such messages get through, as though all the tumblers of a lock have reached position.

Close friend David was given to jokes that, on occasion, passed near the margin of what might usually be told in mixed company. After one such joke, Mother, who had not spoken a word, looked up and said, "Why, David, what would your mother say?" Mother would go weeks without speaking, then all of a sudden, the light would come back. One day in her final year, Missy was sitting by the bed, talking to Mother and stroking her hand. Missy recalled, "She looked at me with clear eyes for just a moment and she said, 'I feel bad because I think I've failed.' I started to cry. 'Honey, it's not your fault,' I said. I felt so sad because that was how she felt."

Such lucid moments were very infrequent. By 2013, Mother could no longer remember the faces of relatives, Jim aside, but she would recognize Dane's voice on greeting cards that allow the sender to record a brief message, maybe not much more than, "Hello, Mother, I love you." The caregivers would play such cards repeatedly. They had a relaxing effect for Mother.

The easiest litany, "Is Jim Dicke your husband?" Mother would respond, "Yes, he is." Then, six months before her death, she could no longer repeat his name. But she continued to recognize his presence, his voice. Caregiver Wendy said, "Yes, she recognized his voice until the end. There were still good days and bad days. There was always a twinkle in her eye when he was around; she was very proud that he was her husband. He was always concerned about her needs first. On her worst days, we made excuses not to put Jim and Eilleen together. Jim needed to see the good days. I think he knew. He would hear the hollering come from her room sometimes, and we would say it was a reaction to water rather than anything more serious. We tried to give him some peace of mind."

Incrementally, Mother was losing control of her muscles. Three-person transfers, with someone under each arm and a third maneuvering the chair, were no longer sufficient for getting her from her bed to her recliner. Four-person transfers became necessary. Such transfers, said Kevin who helped performed them, "weren't easy." Kevin describes the effort involved:

> "I always hated when we had to do a four-person transfer with her. You'd try to get her set up at the foot of the bed. Two people would get her arms. One person would guide her feet and the other would guide the chair with wheels. The transfer was either to a wheelchair or to a commode, and then we would go from there to the recliner. She was dead weight. She had no strength. Mentally, she was unable to grasp what we were trying to do. By the time we got to a four-person transfer, we knew we were near the end with her."

Towards the end, Dani recalled turning away from Mother to make a chart notation, "and she yelled 'Dani!' and I just teared up that she still remembered." Sometimes, Eilleen would go several weeks without enunciating a comprehensible sentence. Then, some months from the end and entirely out of the blue, she turned to Wanda to assure her of "just how much she appreciated everyone's efforts." The comment astounded her longtime friend and caregiver.

Caregiver Wendy's pregnancy overlapped with Mother's final months. Wendy wondered if Mother was aware of the pregnancy. "And a few weeks before she died," Wendy said, "one of the last times she was up in the recliner chair, I was severely pregnant. She didn't say anything, but she smiled at me and reached out and rubbed my belly. She never did that before or after. I wondered if she knew there was a baby there. I really like having that last memory of her."

CHAPTER 17

Death Comes

When Becky walks her dog or stops for a carton of milk, she is reminded that not only is she a pastor, she is a pastor in a small town. In the way of small towns, being out and about means bumping into someone; and if that someone happens to have not recently made it to a pew in New Bremen's St. Paul's United Church of Christ, then some litany of excuse may be forthcoming.

The church is at 119 North Franklin Street, not far from the long-time home of Mother and Dad. Everything in New Bremen is nearby. Becky, the daughter of a pastor, says she-never imagined she would be anything else. Becky was with a youth ministry in Chicago for several years, at a seminary in St. Louis, and then for eleven years at a church in the Dayton suburb of Kettering, co-incidentally near the Webster home. In many denominations, the church is assigned a pastor. In the United Church of Christ, the congregation makes the choice of who shall lead them. Learning of the vacancy in New Bremen, she considered the move, prayed over it, and submitted her portfolio to the church's search committee. In January 2009, she gave a visiting sermon at St. Paul, speaking on the parable of the mustard seed. She began her pastorship the following August.

Becky discovered, after arriving, that she had had unknown ties to New Bremen. Her father was from Wapakoneta, sixteen miles from New Bremen, but forebears had lived in New Bremen first. Her great-grandfather had been baptized in the sanctuary now in her care, and she discovered in town several cousins she had not known. Compared with larger places she had worked, Pastor Becky enjoyed the "small townness" of New Bremen. "I do not miss the traffic, the congestion, or the busy-ness," she said. Her task in New Bremen is somewhat different. "Many families here are multi-generation. In the suburbs, if a member has a crisis, there isn't always family there to help and the church steps in. Here, the church is a part of people's lives during a crisis, but there is also family to offer support."

Dad and Mother were long-time members of St. Paul. In fact, the family had been members since the church was first founded. Pastor Becky paid calls on Dad, and in October 2011, when Mother was having a good day, Becky was introduced to her. She held Mother's hand for a few minutes, then went to take her leave. Becky says, "She held onto my hands firmly, asking me to stay, which I did, and told me that she now considered me a friend." New Bremen was not only multigenerational. Missy brought to Pastor Becky's attention that, with Mother's death, the normal care and attention that would follow needed to be extended to the caregivers as well.

Mother's death came softly, in a year that was still new. During the second week of 2015, she declined further food and water, behavior common to those whose lengthy illness is nearing its end. Carolyn recalled, "It was clear that she wasn't going to be with us much longer." Various caregivers came by to take their leave. Dad, wheelchair-bound, paid a final visit to his wife of seventy-two years. Wendy said, "She just looked bad. Her breathing was bad. We played a recording from the family over and over, and sang to her until the very end. We all took turns going to see her when she was close. I thanked her for taking me into her home and teaching me all those wonderful songs."

On the evening of January 14, Eilleen's blood pressure dropped, her heartbeat declined, and her respiration slowed. Ali was the nurse on duty. Wanda and Kevin were present. Missy was called. I came for a quiet moment with Mother and then to visit with Dad. It was hard.

Mother's bedroom was bathed in the soft light the nurses used during nighttime hours. She was laying on her side, not precisely in a coma, but deeply silently sleeping. She looked exhausted from the struggle she had been through. Rapidly, moments from her life passed through my mind. I remembered her ironing in the kitchen when I was a young boy and setting up card tables for her bridge club. I remembered her playing tennis with my son and how she practically held her breath until I actually became the first family member to get a college degree. I remembered her being always so meticulous about being dressed well. I remembered her joyfully playing the piano and singing. It just all seemed so sad. Dad was in the living room, silently sitting at his table. He was aware of what was going on, was trying not to believe it, and said he was okay. I think Dad really wanted to be alone with his thoughts.

Mother's breathing slowed. One of those present said it seemed like there were minutes between breaths. And some while before midnight, there were no more breaths. The caregivers caucused, commiserated, and concluded it was time to tell Dad that he was now a widower. On receiving the news, Carolyn said, "He was actually pretty calm. He realized that while physically she was now gone; mentally, she had been gone for a while." When the nurses called about Mother's death, I came again. It was all so silent. Mother no longer looked tired. Dad really felt that he could not bear to see her just then. We agreed he should get some sleep. Tomorrow would be a difficult day and we would need to be rested. In the days following, Carolyn added, "Jim would talk about her and cry. It was hard for me to watch. And in the days thereafter, he would mention little things and cry. I would just give him a hug and tell him that she was better off now. It was hard. It was hard."

Mother's memorial service was held in the Dicke home on January 20, 2015. The location was chosen out of concern that Dad, recently hospitalized for pneumonia, not be exposed to the winter elements. The gathering was small—family, caregivers, David and Ruth Ann, Mike from the boat, and a few others came. No one was turned away. The event was intimate, dignified, proper, and casual. For someone who had lived in style, Mother went out in style. She had newly purchased clothing to wear. Mother's long-time hair stylist and manicurist performed those services for the final time. The senior director at the local funeral home handled the arrangements.

Dane later commented, "She was a beautiful woman to start with, and the caregivers did such a good job with her, and the funeral director did such a good job. I thought she was still just that beautiful."

Carol, Mother and Dad's long-time housekeeper, said, "I recall Jim came into their atrium room, which had been converted to a chapel for the service, in a wheelchair. It was very touching; it was his first time seeing her. He was peaceful, because Eilleen had a smile on her face and she looked so nice."

I remember how tightly Dad was trying to control his emotions when he entered the atrium. It was an open casket, then closed for the service. Dad would not approach the casket until both Dane and I were there. Dane was a few minutes late, and when he arrived, Dad was very relieved. I never asked him why he wanted us with him, before he would view Mother. It was almost as if Dad had to have a certain sense of decorum with the husband and sons together for Mother, before he would approach the casket. Perhaps he was just trying hard to keep his composure, and he thought our company would help. For all of us, some losses never really heal. Losing Mother in such a tough way felt even worse.

In the memorial service, Pastor Becky recapitulated the events of Mother's life. The scriptural readings included Proverbs 31:

10-29, which begins, "A capable wife, who can find? She is more special than jewels." The family had decided that Jim III, Eilleen's eldest grandchild, would speak for the family, and then anyone who cared to make comments was welcome to do so.

Jim III's eulogy stuck in the minds of many. He noted, "Some might know her as Gram, some as Nana, some as Mother, or as Eilleen," but all were aware of her humor, her love of music, her affinity with children. She was, he noted, "always interesting, always outgoing... She was the life of the party; she was so much fun." But while she had enjoyed the finer things in life, she had always conveyed a sense of life's proprieties. In her mind, there were lines you were not to cross. Jim Dicke III said later of the event, "We had intentionally made it a small gathering. Gram was so well loved by so many people that had we chosen to do a big thing, there would have been a large number of people. We did what we thought she would have wanted. We also did what we thought would not put Gramp's own life at risk in the cold weather."

Others chose to say a few words. David walked his walker to the front of the room to share a few anecdotes. Monica, Mother's niece, recalled a childhood visit when, affirming that she liked grapefruit, felt special when her Aunt Eilleen presented Monica with a full grapefruit at breakfast time. Caregiver Dani, noting Mike's presence, recalled all the stories she had heard about travelling on the boat, and about how those stories had traveled with Mother back to New Bremen, and had been shared.

There were music selections. Prior to the service, Pastor Becky had learned that Mother's theme song was "Show Me the Way to Go Home." Pastor Becky had not known the song, had to look it up, and realized that it was a somewhat plaintive call for help from someone who had over-imbibed of an evening. Perhaps, she suggested, it could be interpreted to mean going home to the Lord. She didn't know all the words. "Not to worry," Dane said, "we know the song," and everyone did. Carol recalled, "Everybody sang. We'd been hearing that song for so long. Even Jim had a smile."

The other song was "Tea for Two", a favorite of Mother's from an earlier time in her life, when she would change but one lyric. As Mother sang it, the song always said, "a boy for you and a boy for me."

Dad could not accompany Mother to the graveside service, but in the following months he took an active interest in designing their gravestone, confessing that he had never liked the stone his mother had chosen for his father. After their headstone was installed, Dad was driven to the cemetery to see it on a pretty summer's day. One year and ten months after her death, he would join her.

CHAPTER 18

What Next?

With Alzheimer's, as with many things, we look for a cause. What brought this illness? In the case of the Alzheimer's victim, the answer is unsatisfyingly simple: We don't know. How aware is she of her situation? We hope they aren't, but even if they are fleetingly aware, that clarity probably lasts but a moment, or does it? We just don't know.

The question then becomes: What is to be done?

In clinical terms, Alzheimer's research is an area of much activity, but as yet little in the way of a likely fundamental breakthrough rests on the horizon. For the immediate future, the well-being of the increasing number of Alzheimer' sufferers will be determined less by laboratory research than by the Alzheimer's patients themselves and by the skills, attentiveness, and sheer stamina of all those who take on their care. Few of those who take on the care of an Alzheimer's patient will duplicate the labor intensity of the care provided to Mother, but her story illustrates the magnitude, intensity and heartbreak of the challenge. Still, the story in this book hopes to offer value to patients, families, and caregivers.

Recent years have seen an outpouring of writing on the subject—books on research, first-person accounts of caring for an Alzheimer's victim, advice from experts to families of the afflicted. The Alzheimer's Association website is an outstanding resource.

First, as with many medical conditions, the highest emphasis is to be placed on early detection. Here, two obstacles are to be overcome. The first is the altogether understandable reluctance of family members to identify a relative as slipping into Alzheimer's. A diagnosis of Alzheimer's is, for the patient, a sentence of death, but is also for the family, acceptance of a likely enormous emotional and financial demand.

Complicating this is the fact that it is a good deal more difficult to realize someone is facing Alzheimer's than that someone has, say, a broken leg. Some level of memory loss is standard to aging, and the point at which deterioration of memory has passed the point of a normal decline is hardly clear cut. As Mother's neurologist, Dr. Pugar, noted, "Almost everyone begins with 'surplus brain' with more cognitive ability than they require." The symptoms of Alzheimer's do not appear until that surplus is exhausted. "Brain" is a wasting asset; but if we can alter the vector of decline, we can slow it down." The slower the rate of decline, the longer it takes the Alzheimer's patient to drop each step lower on the ladder of capability. "Unfortunately," Dr. Pugar said, "we often don't see people until they can no longer manage their checkbook." What is required is a rising public awareness that the prospective Alzheimer patient is not benefited by disregarding symptoms of decline, and that the earliest possible recognition benefits them.

The next obstacle is within the medical community. All manner of demands press upon a physician's time with a patient. Certain general standards exist in medical practice. For example, after some age, women should have a mammogram; men should have a prostate exam; and all should have a colonoscopy. No such screening standard yet exists for the onset of Alzheimer's, which is considerably more common and generally more debilitating than other diseases where screening is standard. What is needed from the medical practitioner's side is that an annual exam of anyone past, say, the age of fifty-five include a brief series of cognitive tests that might alert the physician to the need for a referral to a neurologist. The patient or an accompanying family member needs to ask that it be done.

One needs to bear in mind that there are two sides to this diagnosis—that of the patient, and that of those who will care for the patient. The earlier the condition is diagnosed, the more the patient can do to postpone its impact.

For their part, caregivers face a heavy burden. According to the Alzheimer's Association's 2014 Facts and Figures Report, in 2013 more than 15.5 million caregivers nationally devoted 17.7 billion hours of uncompensated care—an average of twenty hours a week, each. Of these, three in five rated their own emotional stress level as either high or very high. Dr. Pugar noted that as his years of treating Alzheimer's patients pass, his attention starts to shift to the caregivers... How are they bearing up under the strain of the disease? What do they need?

To those faced with caring for a family member, Missy stresses, "First, you are not alone. Many others near where you live are engaged in similar struggles. Seek a support group. The road is going to be tough, but it's going to be okay."

As an individual's memory fades, his access to his own past, to his experiences and the multiple meanings that attach to things, is also diminished.

The world of an Alzheimer's patient is a constantly shrinking one. The ability to cope with even minor change decreases. Routine becomes paramount.

It is also important not to argue. As memory deteriorates, the sufferer clings to individual pieces of memory like so many floating pieces of ice, tiny and safe in a vast and threatening sea. Pointing out where they are mistaken only hastens their decline.

Change the subject. This process is known as redirection. In the case of Mother, it commonly consisted of redirecting her distressed attention to some more pleasant topic—her husband, her larger family, trips she may have taken or places she may have visited.

Do not take the illness personally. As Mother's illness progressed, I learned that people get upset by the loss of cognition in someone they love. It can be baffling. Is she telling the truth, in the sense of being honest, or is what she is saying a consequence of the illness? Some say that a person, when drunk, is telling a truth that good manners prevent him from telling when sober. True or not in the case of alcohol, it is not true in the case of Alzheimer's. You are not hearing some long brooded over truth; rather, you are hearing the sputterings of a damaged brain. Alzheimer's does not free people to speak harsh truths.

Mother's early years were burdened by her mother's manic depression. Her father, successful in business, sensible in outlook, sincere in concern, sought repeatedly for the path that would bring peace to his wife and to the family. In that search he did not seek out faddish approaches or quack cures, but he sought the state of the art that was meant to bring peace. Peace, peace, but there was no peace. There was no peace because in the 1930s and 1940s, no treatment for manic depression was yet to be found.

For many years, Mother was burdened by the progressive deterioration that came to her with Alzheimer's disease. It is, here again, fair to say that no intelligent resource was spared to lessen her burden and lighten her days. The limit was not set by lack of funds, lack of compassion, or lack of informed will. The limit was set by the simple determination of Alzheimer's disease to tie her brain into countless knots and bundles. Generally effective treatments for manic depression exist today. A generally effective prevention or cure for Alzheimer's is being sought. Born in 1921, died in 2015, Mother led a life whose years were bookended by matters that two educated and resourceful families could not reverse, not for effort, not for love, and not for money. Limits exist. The race is not always to the swift, nor wisdom to the wise, but time and chance will be with us always and bring us better days. For now, we row on against the tide.

Family Mentioned by Name

1. Winifred Eilleen Webster Dicke, "Eilleen"—The main character
2. Jim Dicke—Eilleen's husband
3. Warren and Mary Adams Webster—Eilleen's parents
4. Dorothy and Doris—Eilleen's fraternal twin sisters
5. Warren II (Sunny)—Eilleen's brother
6. Monica—Eilleen's niece (Warren II's daughter)
7. Carl and Irene Kamman Dicke—Eilleen's parents-in-law (Jim's parents)
8. Henry and Emma Mauer Dicke—Jim's paternal grandparents
9. Fred and Margaret Foth Kamman—Jim's fraternal grandparents
10. Edna and Mary—Jim's sisters
11. Jim II—Eilleen's elder son (the author)
12. Janet St. Clair Dicke—Eilleen's daughter-in-law (Jim II's spouse)
13. Jim III and Jennifer—Children to Jim II and Janet Dicke
14. Dane Webster Dicke —Eilleen's younger son
15. Kerry Sexton Dicke —Eilleen's daughter-in-law (Dane's first wife)
16. Cindy Thomas Dicke—Eilleen's daughter-in-law (Dane's second wife)
17. Anastasia and Robin—Children to Dane and Kerry Dicke
18. Lucile—Jim Dicke's cousin

Caregivers and Associates Mentioned by Name

1. Dr. David Imler—Eilleen and Jim Dicke's medical care coordination
2. Dr. David Louis—Eilleen and Jim Dicke's medical care coordination
3. Dr. Kenneth Pugar—Eilleen's neurologist
4. Missy—A caregiver to Eilleen and Jim
5. Wanda—A caregiver to Eilleen and Jim
6. Wendy—A caregiver to Eilleen and Jim
7. Rebekkah—A caregiver to Eilleen and Jim
8. Dani—A caregiver to Eilleen and Jim
9. Carolyn—A caregiver to Eilleen and Jim
10. Rachel—A caregiver to Eilleen and Jim
11. Ali—A caregiver to Eilleen and Jim
12. Dan—A caregiver to Eilleen and Jim
13. Kevin—A caregiver to Eilleen and Jim
14. Julie F.—Hair care provider to Eilleen and Jim
15. Julia M—Hair care provider to Eilleen and Jim
16. Carol—Housekeeper/caregiver to Eilleen and Jim
17. Becky—Pastor to Eilleen and Jim (St. Paul's Church)

Friends and Associates Mentioned by Name

1. Julie—Executive Assistant to Jim II
2. Kathy—Crown Executive who helped with family business matters
3. David and Ruth Ann Schwieterman—Eilleen and Jim's friends
4. Jim and Nedie Moeller—Eilleen and Jim's friends
5. Margaret—Eilleen's friend
6. Eddie Steppe—Childhood friend of Eilleen and Jim
7. Tom Bidwell—Crown Executive
8. Verlin Hirschfeld—Crown Executive
9. Zita—Eilleen's friend (Tom Bidwell's spouse)
10. Mike—Captain of Eilleen and Jim's boat
11. Francis "Oxi" Oxrider—Salesperson friend to Eilleen (Grandmother to Cindy Thomas Dicke)
12. Everett "E.P." Larsh—President of the Master Electric Company, one-time employer of Carl Dicke and briefly of Jim Dicke; owner of a yacht admired by Jim Dicke
13. Reverend Gruenwald—Pastor who married Eilleen and Jim
14. Molly—Clarence "Molly" Woerman, the town policeman in 1950s
15. Mark Bernstein—Friend of Jim II (gifted interviewer and writer)
16. Francis—An imaginary tormentor of Eilleen